THE VEIL
IS TORN!

Why You Can Break Out of The Prison of Religion, Drop Your Cross, take up his glory And Start Enjoying Your New Life in Jesus Christ...

GREAT IGWE

WIGE PUBLISHING MEDIA
New York- Lagos- Virginia

THE VEIL IS TORN
© 2020 By GREAT IGWE

Unless otherwise noted, scriptures quotations are from the Holy Bible, King James version (KJV) ©1979-1980-1982-1984 by Thomas Nelson, Inc. used by permission. All rights reserved new international version (NIV), ©1973-1978-1984 by the international Bible Society. Used by permission of Zondervan. Scripture quotations marked (NASB) are taken from New American Standard Bible. Scripture quotation marked (ESV) are taken from the English Standard Version with permission from Good News Publisher.

First Published 2020

ISBN: Hardcover: **978-1-7332803-4-1**. eBook: **978-1-7332803-3-4**.

Published and printed in the United State of America by: WEGI Publishing House and Distributed by Amazon and Ingramspark.

www.WegiGroup.com

Library of Congress Control Number: 2020909957

WEGI Publishing House is a Subsidiary of the WEGI Group, Inc. The WEGI Publishing House Name and Logo are trademarks of WEGI Group, Inc. Quantity sales. Special discounts are available on quantity purchases by corporations, associations, and others. For details, contact the publisher at the address above. Email: infor@wegigroup.com. *Tel; +1 (240)-688-2092*

PRAISES FOR THE VEIL IS TORN

The Veil Is Torn is a passionate and inspiring look at God's marvelous love in providing access to Himself through the cross of Jesus. This book will change your life, not only in understanding our place before God but in empowering us as believers to better explain these principles to others. It is riveting to look at what it means to walk through the curtain of God's free gift of salvation, into the Holy of Holies of God's presence not because of our goodness, but because of his unwavering love for us as His children. Get ready to be captivated and inspired.

David Johnson

CEO, PermaLast Coating Systems

This book made me question everything I know about religion. Having been born in the Catholic faith myself, I have held (and still hold) onto some things that have been engrained by priests and other religious leaders even though they add little to no value in my walk. Is just what it is because "they" said. I love how "Great Igwe" appears to challenge/debunk these apocryphal teachings and, more importantly, leads one on a journey to understand, accept and yet dissect everything!

Jessica Okeze,o

Human Resources Specialist @ Freshly Inc.

The veil is torn is a must read for anyone who is interested in advancing his/her knowledge in the finished work of Christ. The book provides a clear, well-structured exposition of the finished work of Christ. Mr. Great point out words we hear less and less about in the modern church age. The Veil is Torn is an engaging read that explains God's will for our time. Great Igwe has written a diamond among a sea of books and this would make an important addition to anyone's library and is a wonderful personal study.

Joe Otobo

CEO Becjoe Media LTD

Great Igwe sets himself apart as a writer in that he seeks to empower his audience without putting them through any elaborate mental gymnastics. By showcasing the simplicity of the Gospel and Christ's work on the cross, he strips away the misunderstandings that often surround the Christian faith to reveal the heart of the Father. Whether you're a long-time believer or new to the faith, this book is sure to encourage and strengthen you in its presentation of the simple truth of God's love and the freedom we now walk in as Christians.

Rebecca Masamitsu,

Chi Alpha Missionary

If I was asked to recommend a book every bible-based church should have, it will be this book "The Veil is Torn". In my 26 years of pastoring, this is the first time the topic of tithing and fasting has been excellently explained in context holistically.

Bishop Michael Mcweaver

President, Northhill Church Orlando

An incredible in-depth, study of who we are as believers! We are not meant to feel defeated or guilty or hopeless. This dense but easy to follow journey will help you redefine your identity to understand that you are a loved and accepted child of God.

Ashley Johnson

Department of Homeland Security

It is said that Portland is the place where 30-year old's come to retire. The Veil is Torn by Great Igwe shows that Jesus is where ALL come to retire whether they know it or not.

Scot Moonfiled

Snr. Pastor Oaktree Assembly. Canada

This is one of the most clearly stated and detailed writings about the finished work of Jesus Christ. Pastor Great, has masterfully discredit the false religious assumptions and explanation on salvation in such an incredible way. From the first to the last chapter, will leave you amazed.

Dr Byion Copper Jnr

Country Director, Red-Cross

The construction of the Book meshes well with it's organization and lends itself successfully to the Author's hard work of research and application. I believe this is a book that will be a lifelong manual for anyone with a passion for the "Truth that sets one free" These things are written to stir up a passion in each of our lives for the tomorrows that hold great promise and Revolution!

Evangelist Keshia R. Freeland

Founder/President LoveAflame Intl.

Appreciation

To God the Father who gives all wisdom and knowledge to His children. Special thanks to Ashley my partner and best pal, for being my confidant and sounding board. Your love and care for me girl, is unmatched. To all members of my editorial and production team, I'm grateful for all the time and patience you guys gave to this work. Lastly. I would like to acknowledge Dr Abel Damina and Andrew Wommack, men whose teachings have greatly inspired me.

CONTENTS

INTRODUCTION

The fall of man in the Garden of Eden gave birth to the ultimate loss of fellowship of Man with God. Man became sundered from God in his mind and lost the awareness of his immortal relationship with His Creator. He misplaced his identity, his rights, and his privileges and became a slave in a realm he was originally to dominate and control. This rebellion introduced the Sin "Nature" in Man and marked the beginning of his sufferings and ultimate spiritual death.

As I ponder on this, I can't help but wonder if the "fall of man" in the Garden took God by surprise. Of course, that is a capital NO. As the Omnibenevolent, Omniscient, and Omnipotent Loving Father God planned that Jesus would die for Mankind's sins. The Scripture boldly declares that Jesus is the Lamb that was slain before the foundation of the earth.

Until Christ's death, God set in place a system where animal sacrifices had to be offered for the partial covering or reparation of Man's sin in the old covenant. It was complicated, expensive, and a great burden in the life of Man. People sinned every day, just as we do now, and so these sacrifices were offered yearly for atonement or based on the specific spiritual needs of the people.

The old covenant is a sort of agreement between Man and God. It can be likened to a *quid pro quo* agreement, which simply means to get this, you must do that. Man needed to keep the commandments in order for God to bless him, forgive his sins, and, hopefully, gain eternal life after death. The old covenant was a covenant filled with dos and don'ts. Believe me, it was not funny at all.

Man, who originally had an intimate fellowship with God in the garden, could not even enter the Holy Place of the Temple. He needed a high priest to intercede on his behalf. All he knew about God was subject to what the priest and prophet could reveal to him, which were subject to personal interpretation or opinions of prophets who also had never seen God themselves.

He was completely lost and could not redeem himself. All he could do was offer sacrifices of rams, goat, bulls, and turtle doves to atone for his sins, but all these animal sacrifices could do was cover Man's sins. Man was still alienated from his Maker.

Man was created in the image and likeness of God, with His full glory and authority. Satan made Man doubt who he was, and he fell for it in what I call the "Identity Deception" – the highest deception of all ages. With the fall, Man became lost, and all he began doing from that day forward was geared towards finding his true purpose and identity.

The search for redemption, relationship, and identity by Man gave birth to all kinds of false doctrines, religious rituals, and practices that have enslaved the old Man. Many religious lords and false prophets have used ignorance and crisis in Man to enslave and extort the ignorant man.

These religious masters have intelligently used Man's ignorance of the Scripture to put him on a never-ending quest of trying to save himself through works. But the more Man tries to save himself by his works, the more frustrated he becomes. Why? because he always ends up doing the things he vows to not do again. Since he cannot stop, he simply becomes a hypocrite.

The birth, death, and resurrection of Jesus Christ is the greatest miracles for Man and God's ultimate Gift to mankind. With Christ's death and resurrection, God redeemed mankind back to Himself once and for all – not through the blood of animals that could only cover Man's sins temporarily but through the precious blood of His begotten Son Jesus Christ. With the death of Jesus, Man now has a new life, a new spirit, and above all, the precious gift of salvation.

With the death of Christ, the Veil that separated Man from God was torn. There is, therefore, no condemnation to Man if he believes in Christ. Man is now a mobile temple of the embodiment of the Godhead. He needs no mediator, no more animal sacrifice for the atonement of sins. Rather, with this new life, his past, present, and future sins are forgiven.

With the removal of this Veil, Man gained direct relationship with his Maker. In fact, this new relationship is even better than what the first man experienced in the Garden of Eden. The first man had God visit him periodically, but this new, recreated man has God residing inside him forever. What an intimate relationship!!! It's my desire that through this book, you will:

- Come to the knowledge of the unchangeable love of God towards you.

- Understand the significance of the death, burial, and resurrection of Jesus Christ in your life.

- Break out of the shackles and bondage of religion.

- Above all, get a glimpse into the true nature and personality of God and hopefully distinguish it from the frequent lie's religion has told you about Him. Get ready to unlearn to relearn. Enjoy the ride!!!

CHAPTER 1

LIFE BEFORE THE CROSS

Life before the cross was life in which Man was trying to please God through his ability to keep the commandments. It was life lived on the foundation of the old covenant. It was a life filled with faithlessness and ignorance of Man's rights as God's children. Life before the cross was life in which we were "fools" living like slaves when we were destined and created to reign as princes and princesses. Life before the cross was a life of God dwelling in temples and the ark of the covenant.

A careful study of the Old Testament reveals the hopelessness we were under due to lack of faith. As I studied the Old Testament, I noticed that most of the people that God had a closer relationship with were people who walked in faith: Abraham, David, Esther, Solomon, and lot more. Life before the Cross was a life built on lies and showmanship; it was a life filled with the blood of animals. Indeed, such a life was not the kind of life God destined for us. We brought it upon ourselves.

In order to appreciate the new life, we have in Christ, it's pertinent that we look back on how we got here, the price that was paid on our behalf, and the sufferings Man went through trying to please God based on works. In chapters one and two, I will try to explain some common aspects of the Old Testament relationship with God.

Why the Animal sacrifice?

God required animal sacrifices in the Old Testament to demonstrate the severity of sin, the cost of rebellion against God, the death that sin brings, and the cost that must be paid to be redeemed.

The sacrifices served as a kind of placeholder while people waited for the true Messiah to come and the true sacrifice to be offered. After all, the blood of animals cannot cleanse Man from sin. So, the Old Testament animal sacrifices were a representation of the death of Christ on the cross that would later occur, and which was recorded in the Gospels.

Hebrews 10:1-3 (NASB) reads, *For the Law, since it has only a shadow of the good things to come and not the very form of things, can never, by the same sacrifices which they offer continually year by year, make perfect those who draw near. Otherwise, would they not have ceased to be offered, because that the worshippers, having once been cleansed would no longer have had consciousness of sins? But in those sacrifices, there is a reminder made of sins year by year.*

In the Old Testament, the bloodshed was necessary because God told us in Leviticus 17:11 (NASB), "For the life of the flesh is in the blood, and I have given it to you on the altar to make atonement for your souls; for it is the blood by reason of the life that makes atonement." Atonement is a cleansing, a removal of sin. So, animal sacrifices were a temporary means by which atonements could occur that would "cleanse" people of their sins. They were fulfilled in Christ, and with Him, no further animal sacrifices were necessary.

Hebrews 9:11-14 (NASB) reads, *"But when Christ appeared as a high priest of the good things to come, He entered through the greater and more perfect tabernacle, not made with hands, that is to say, not of this creation; and not through the blood of goats and calves, but through His own blood. He entered the holy place once for all, having obtained eternal redemption. For if the blood of goats and bulls and the ashes of a heifer sprinkling those who have been defiled sanctify for the cleansing of the flesh, how much more will the blood of Christ, who through the eternal Spirit offered Himself without blemish to God, cleanse your conscience from dead works to serve the living God".*

Jesus is the entire message of the Bible.
He is the summary and central theme of the Bible.

In the Old Testament, to be in God's holy presence, Man had to be without sin because God is Holy (1 Peter 1:16). When a person sins, there is a consequence for breaking the Law of God. That consequence is death and separation from God. On the cross, Jesus bore our sins in His body. Another way of looking at it is that He "became sin," though He never committed sin.

When Jesus died on the cross, the Law of God was satisfied; this is justice. But because God is merciful and gracious, He extends that death, that atoning sacrifice to all who would receive it by faith, so all believers are made right before God. With Christ's death, a new covenant was instituted. Hebrew 9:15 (NASB) reads, *And for this reason He is the mediator of a new covenant, so that, since a death has taken place for the redemption of the transgressions that were committed under the first covenant, those who have been called may receive the promise of the eternal inheritance".*

Therefore, because Jesus died on the cross, we had a new covenant, a new contract with God where God gives us the righteousness of Christ and deliverance from eternal judgment.

How God Communicated to Us Before the Cross

Throughout the Old Testament, God spoke to mankind through visions, dreams, shadows, angelic visitations, and pictures. But these communications were mostly between God and His prophets. These prophets then relayed this message to the people based on their understanding of the message. *"God, who at sundry times and in divers manners spoke in time past unto the fathers by the prophets, Hath in these last days spoken unto us by his Son, whom He hath appointed heir of all things, by whom also He made the worlds".(Hebrew 1:1-2)*

When properly interpreted, these verses mean: "At various times, in different ways, the prophets spoke to our fathers, but in these last days, God has spoken through His Son." This Scripture explains how God communicated in the Old Testament and how He spoke in the New Testament.

The speaking was through the revelation of a person. A prophet hears, then says. Every time the Bible refers to the prophet speaking, it doesn't say God spoke, but rather the prophet spoke about what he knew and understood about God. The prophets spoke in Hebrews 1:1; God spoke in verse 2. Before the cross, Man revealed and interpreted, so all the prophets said could never have been complete, and what they communicated was imperfect.

In the second verse, however, God has spoken by His Son. That message is given once. It shows finality. That is, the summary of all the prophets said was the Son. He is the arrival point, the summation of all they said. It was the prophets who spoke in different portions of truth and in different manners unto the fathers while God's revelation is the Son.

The Bible is a book of progressive revelation beginning at Genesis, segmented into the Old and New Testament. The Old Testament is referred to as "the Scriptures" in the New Testament.

Luke 24:27 *reads, "And beginning at Moses, and all the prophets he expounded unto them in all the scriptures the things concerning himself".*

Matthew 13:11 reads, *"He answered and said unto them, because it is given unto you to know the mysteries of the kingdom of heaven, but to them it is not given".*

Mark 4:11 reads – *"And he said unto them, Unto you it is given to know the mystery of the kingdom of God: but unto them that are without, all these things are done in parables".*

The word mystery implies something hidden, a secret, something to be explained. Paul also describes the Old Testament as mysteries in Rom. 16:25-26: *Now to him that is of the power to stablish you according to my gospel, and the preaching of Jesus Christ, according to the revelation of the mystery, which was kept secret since the world began, But now is made manifest, and by the scriptures of the prophets, according to the commandment of the everlasting God, made known to all nations for the obedience of faith.*

Notice he said, "kept secret." It shows that the Scriptures concealed things. The Scriptures required explanation. The book of Colossians made this clearer. *"Even the mystery which hath been hid from ages and from generations, but now is made manifest to his saints."* (Colossians 1:26).

n the Old Testament, Jesus is concealed in types and shadows, prophesies, and promises, while in the New Testament books, Jesus is revealed – or Jesus manifest. Peter described the prophets as investigating, seeking after; that is, they were asking questions in their utterances and prophecies. 1 Peter 1:9-11 reads, *"Receiving the end of your faith, even the salvation of your souls. Of which salvation the prophets have enquired and searched diligently, who prophesied of the grace that should come unto you: Searching what, or what manner of time the Spirit of Christ which was in them did signify, when it testified beforehand the sufferings of Christ, and the glory that should follow".*

From this Scripture, we know that the full explanation of what the Old Testament prophets said cannot be found in their writings. The Spirit in them testified of Christ's sufferings and the glory to come. Therefore, in the scriptures Christ is hidden and concealed. Hebrews 10:1reads, *"For the law having a shadow of good things to come, and not the very image of the things, can never with those sacrifices which they offered year by year continually make the comers thereunto perfect".*

The writer of Hebrews describes the law as a shadow. The word "shadow" means 'darkness, thick darkness.' There is no light in darkness, and nothing can be seen in darkness. But we are under a new covenant and are no longer in darkness. I boldly say that God speaks to every one of His children in this new dispensation. If you are a believer, you have the express authority and right to communicate with God and hear Him communicate back to you. This is one of the rights and privileges that comes with your salvation.

Your pastor or bishop or prophet is not the only mouthpiece or representative of God on earth. We are all God's representatives on earth. You are a mouthpiece of God. You are a priest of God. Religion has made us believe that our church leaders are the sole voice of God on earth. This is a lie and it's not scriptural.

Every believer is a voice of God on earth. This doesn't mean that our church leaders are not hearing from God. No. They do. What I am trying to communicate to you is the fact that you also are worthy to hear from God. God is speaking to you and through you.

God still talks to people.

Okay Great, why don't I hear God speak to me?

Many believers feel as though God doesn't speak to them or they cannot hear God due to three factors.

1. ***Wrong religious teachings:*** There are many churches today that don't believe that God still speaks to His children. Some also believe that God peaks only through the general overseer of the church or senior pastor or bishop. Some have been taught that certain revelation can only be revealed to the general overseer of the church. This is just not true. The same Holy Spirit living in your pastor is the same Spirit living in you. Thus, the remedy to this falsehood is to renew your mind from such wrong teachings as we were admonished in Romans 12:2.

2. ***Insensitivity to the leading of the Holy Spirit:*** This is another major reason why many believers don't hear God. The truth is that God is speaking to us every second. Through friends, through our parents, through our church leaders, through that inner voice, through our visions and dreams. He also speaks loudly for us to hear. To me, most of the time, God has spoken through the leading in my mind and inner voice.

The question is not whether God is speaking,
It's whether you're listening

Have you ever been in a position where you were about to do something, but you keep getting this cold, weird feeling to not do it? Or you keep struggling to do it. Sometimes in that moment, it seems your entire body is on fire or your entire being is against it? Friend, that's the Holy Spirit talking to you. As a believer, you must be sensitive to the presence of the Holy Spirit and His interactions with you.

The Holy Spirit did not just come to live in you and do nothing. He is there to help you have a successful life on earth as a believer. He is your closest friend. A companion, a gossip mate. He communicates with you daily. Learn to know when He is saying No or Yes. Ask Him. Live your life with this expectation and knowledge.

3. ***Lack of studying the Bible:*** The Word of God is absolute and infallible. Therefore, it's the ultimate source of the voice of God for anyone desiring to hear Him. The words contained in the Bible were inspired by God. Whatever spiritual knowledge you seek is contained in the Bible: How-to live-in peace in your community, how to treat your neighbors.

The Word of God describes the person of God, His love, and His will for your life.

The Bible is the absolute and infallible word of God.

Every truth you will ever seek is found in the Bible. To understand the Bible, you must read it with the revelation of the person of Christ. You must interpret it through the knowledge of Jesus Christ, who is the express image and embodiment of God.

You cannot afford to read the Scriptures as you would your newspaper or social media. You must understand what is being said in every verse of the Bible, why it's being said, when it's being said, and to whom (i.e. the pre-context, context, and post-context). It's also crucial that you take into consideration the cultural norms or traditions of the people being addressed in any passage of the Bible. This will help you to understand the lesson or point.

You also must differentiate between words that are added by Bible translators for better understanding and words that are part of the original collation. Finally, you must differentiate between life in the Old Testament and that in the New Testament and depend on the Holy Spirit to reveal His word to you. Not everything said by your church leader is from God. Not everything said from the pulpit is scriptural. It's your duty as a believer to go home, sit down, and dissect the message through the lens of grace and the Epistles. If during your personal study, there is a word or message that is not in agreement with the Epistles and teachings of Christ, discard it. The next chapter is where things get even more interesting.

CHAPTER 2

THE TEMPLE AND THE ARK OF THE COVENANT

We cannot understand Old Testament life (i.e. life before the Cross) without studying the significance of the Temple and the Ark of the Covenant. These two traditions played a major role in the Old Testament world.

I will try to shed some light on questions like this: What did the temple represent to the Old Testament saints. What does the Ark symbolize? Why was the high priest the only one who had access to the innermost court (room) of the temple? What is in the Ark of the Covenant and what does it represent? Why did the Veil of Temple tear apart the moment Jesus Christ died on the cross?

What is the Ark of the Covenant?

Have you ever wondered what the Ark of the Covenant was? What was its purpose? Was it real? Why is it in the Bible? The Ark of the Covenant was a sacred chest built by the Israelites with exact specifications given by God. The Ark was God's pledge that He would dwell among His people and give them guidance from the mercy seat on the top of the Ark.

The Ark was an important foreshadowing of Jesus Christ as the sole place of atonement for sins. The Ark represented the presence of God because the contents reflected God's nature and His attributes of faithfulness, holiness, and sustaining of life for those who are His own.

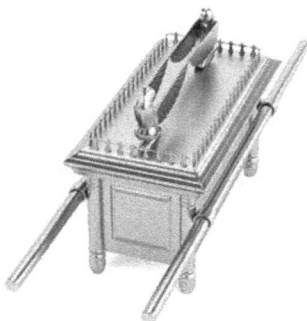

When the Philistines captured the Ark (1 Samuel 4:11), God's glory was said to have departed from Israel, but the Philistines suffered from several plagues when they had the Ark among them. When Israel crossed the Jordan River with the Ark, the waters miraculously stopped, and Israel was able to cross over on dry ground.

The significance of the water being stopped is that water sometimes represents God's judgment, and when God is present and a person or a nation lives in obedience to Him, the judgment of God is withheld. The many historical accounts in the Bible clearly show that the Ark of the Covenant was real and not fictitious, even though no one knows where it is today.

The Ark's Contents

The Ark of the Covenant contained relics that reflected God's holiness and His faithfulness. Inside of the Ark were two tablets of the Decalogue (or the Ten Commandments), a pot containing manna, and Aaron's rod. The tablets symbolize that God is a holy God and requires obedience to His law. The manna was food from the days when God miraculously sustained Israel in the wilderness. The manna in the Ark points to Jesus being the Bread from Heaven and the Bread of Life.

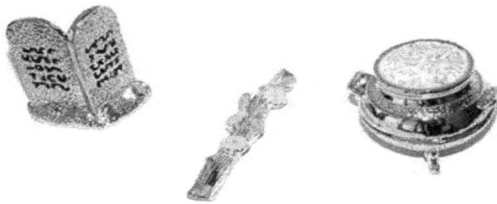

Aaron's rod spoke of God's sovereignty in choosing leaders, showing that leadership must come from God and not from Man (Numbers 17). Men do not choose themselves to be saved and placed into Spiritual leadership positions but are chosen by God.

The Ark also contained the Pentateuch, the first five books of the Old Testament, written by Moses. The Ark represented the presence of God, and by their careful treatment and handling of the Ark, Israel had to be strict in their adherence of all that God required so they might live (1 Samuel 4:11; 2 Samuel 6:7).

The Ark's Symbolic Meaning

The Ark of the Covenant was placed within a special room in the Temple called the Holy of Holies. Only the high priest could have access to this room, and then, only once a year (on the Day of Atonement or Yom Kippur). Anyone that came into contact with the Ark, besides the high priest, would instantly die because no one can see God and live.

The Ark and the Temple are earthly symbols of the heavenly sanctuary. The top, or lid, of the Ark was appropriately called the Mercy Seat and represented the Lamb of God by Whom we have all obtained mercy. The lid had two golden cherubim angels which protected the Ark, just as a cherub angel guarded the Garden of Eden and prohibited Man from returning and partaking of the Tree of Life once Adam and Eve had fallen. These two cherubim protected and magnified God's glory.

When the high priest entered the Holy of Holies on the Day of Atonement, he sprinkled animal blood over the Ark, foreshadowing Christ's blood that would be shed for the remission of sins. At that time, the sacrificial blood only *covered* the people's sins but could never take them away (Hebrews 10:4-11). But when Christ shed His own blood, He took away the sins of those who trusted in Him.

This was where the blood and the mercy of God (on the Mercy Seat) meet in the form of the blood of the Lamb of God, shed for us who have repented and trusted in Him. We get what we do not deserve (called grace) while not getting what we truly do deserve (called mercy).

Christ Blood is God Mercy

In the Book of Hebrews, we see how the Ark was a shadow of things to come, but now the reality is here in the form of Jesus Christ, who is God. Instead of a finite, imperfect, human high priest. The scripture reads in Hebrews 9:11-14 (ESV), *"When Christ appeared as a high priest of the good things that have come, then through the greater and more perfect tent (not made with hands, that is, not of this creation) he entered once for all into the holy places, not by means of the blood of goats and calves but by means of his own blood, thus securing an eternal redemption. For if the blood of goats and bulls, and the sprinkling of defiled persons with the ashes of a heifer, sanctify for the purification of the flesh, how much more will the blood of Christ, who through the eternal Spirit offered himself without blemish to God, purify our conscience from dead works to serve the living God".*

Worshipping God in the Old Testament, (before the cross) had stringent restrictions and regulations. The book of Hebrews gave us a clear look into such regulations.

Hebrews 9:1-10 (ESV) reads, *Now even the first covenant had regulations for worship and an earthly place of holiness. For a tent was prepared, the first section, in which were the lampstand and the table and the bread of the Presence. It is called the Holy Place. Behind the second curtain was a second section called the Most Holy Place, having the golden altar of incense and the ark of the covenant covered on all sides with gold, in which was a golden urn holding the manna, and Aaron's staff that budded, and the tablets of the covenant. Above it was the cherubim of glory overshadowing the mercy seat. Of these things we cannot now speak in detail. These preparations having thus been made, the priests go regularly into the first section, performing their ritual duties, but into the second only the high priest goes, and he but once a year, and not without taking blood, which he offers for himself and for the unintentional sins of the people. By this the Holy Spirit indicates that the way into the holy places is not yet opened as long as the first section is still standing (which is symbolic for the present age). According to this arrangement, gifts and sacrifices are offered that cannot perfect the conscience of the worshiper, but deal only with food and drink and various washings, regulations for the body imposed until the time of reformation.*

The Temple Veil's Purpose

The veil was a long, woven curtain made to separate the Holy of Holies (or Most Holy Place) – which held the Ark of the Covenant and the Mercy Seat – from the rest of the Temple. Only the High Priest could enter this Most Holy Place and only once a year, on the Day of Atonement, after going through a ritual of cleansing. Sitting on top of the Ark was a gold lid. This was the place for the propitiation of sins by the sprinkling of the innocent sacrifice's blood. Propitiation simply means the appeasing of the wrath of God for the sins of Mankind. It provided satisfaction for sin.

Diagram of the Temple

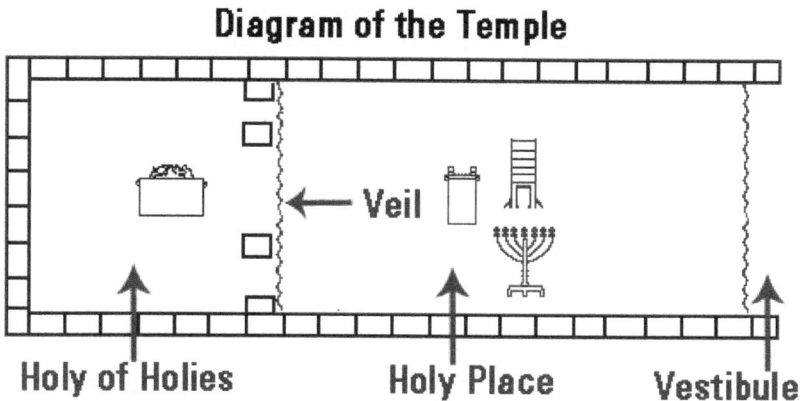

Holy of Holies   **Holy Place**   **Vestibule**

Figure 1: An illustration of the Temple outlining the various sections in the Temple including the Holy of Holies, the veil separating the Holy of Holies, the Ark of the Covenant and the entrance into the Temple.

If anyone simply walked behind the veil, and they were not the High Priest or if the High Priest entered on a day other than the Day of Atonement, that person would immediately die. The veil was a protection against a casual or accidental infringement upon the Most Holy Place, which represented the very real presence of God.

No one could look at God and live (Exodus 33:20) because He is a consuming fire (Deuteronomy 4:24; Hebrews 12:29). The Shekinah-glory that was shining above the Mercy Seat would annihilate anyone but the High Priest, and so the temple's veil protected humans from instant death.

The veil was a symbol of the separation between God and sinful Mankind. It marked the boundary between God's pure holiness and the Mankind's wickedness. Man could not go beyond the veil because our sins separated us from a Holy God. The profane and the Holy cannot be joined.

During Jesus' lifetime, the holy temple in Jerusalem was the center of Jewish religious life. The temple was the place where animal sacrifices were carried out, and worship according to the law of Moses was followed faithfully. Hebrews 9:1-9 tells us that in the temple a veil separated the Holy of Holies – the earthly dwelling place of God's presence – from the rest of the Temple, where Man dwelt.

This signified that Man was separated from God by sin (Isaiah 59:1-2). Like we saw above, only the high priest was permitted to pass beyond this veil once each year (Exodus 30:10; Hebrews 9:7) to enter God's presence for all of Israel and make atonement for their sins (Leviticus 16).

Solomon's temple was 30 cubits high as recorded in 1Kings 6:2, but Herod had increased the height to 40 cubits, according to the writings of Josephus, a first century Jewish historian. There is uncertainty as to the exact measurement of a cubit, but given the approximate height of the temple, it is safe to assume that the veil was about 60 feet high. Early Jewish tradition says the veil was about four inches thick, but the Bible does not confirm that measurement. The book of Exodus teaches that this thick veil was fashioned from blue, purple, and scarlet material and fine twisted linen.

The size and thickness of the veil make the events of Jesus' death on the cross so much more momentous. Matthew 27:50-51, (NIV) reads. *"And when Jesus had cried out again in a loud voice, he gave up his spirit. At that moment the curtain of the temple was torn in two from top to bottom.".*

The Significance of the Torn Veil in the Temple

The significance of the veil being torn from the top down, and the fact that it was torn, is that Jesus' sacrifice makes it possible for us to come to God the Father boldly. Our sins past, present, or future no longer separate us from Him. Today those who put their trust in Jesus have access to God. 2 Corinthians 5:21 explains that *"God made him who had no sin to be sin for us, so that in him we might become the righteousness of God."*.

The fact is that Jesus Himself was torn for our sakes (Isaiah 53). Our High Priest today is Jesus Christ, who continues to intercede for the saints. Jesus Hebrews 7:21 (NIV) reads; *"became a priest with an oath when God said to him: 'The Lord has sworn and will not change his mind: "You are a priest forever."*(). Because of this oath, Jesus has become the guarantor of a better covenant.

There have been many High Priests, since death prevented them from continuing in office; but because Jesus lives forever, He has a permanent priesthood.

Therefore, He can save completely those who come to God through Him by faith, because He always lives to intercede for them. Such a High Priest truly meets our need—One who is holy, blameless, pure, set apart from sinners, exalted above the heavens.

Unlike the other high priests, He does not need to offer sacrifices day after day, first for His own sins, and then for the sins of the people. He sacrificed for their sins once for all when He offered Himself. Because of Jesus we now have access to the very throne of God. The moment Jesus breathed His last breath, the temple veil was rent. God Himself tearing the veil symbolized the fact that mankind's separation from God had been removed by Jesus' supreme sacrifice at Calvary.

*Jesus died to bring
the barrier down.*

Since Jesus was without blemish, without sin, and kept the Law perfectly for us, His death was the propitiation or satisfaction of the wrath of God against humanity's sins. Isaiah 59:2 declares that *"your iniquities [or sins], have separated you from your God; your sins have hidden his face from you, so that he will not hear."* (NIV). Now that Jesus' once and for all sacrifice was given, we have access to the very throne of God. Before, He would not even hear us, not to mention allow us to approach Him.

The veil was not a small curtain like you see in some movies. The veil was sixty feet tall, thirty feet wide, and four inches thick. The veil was so massive and heavy that in the exaggerated numbers of the times as reported in the Talmud, it took 300 priests to manipulate it. An important point here is that no one could simply tear the veil themselves. It would take more than human strength to tear it. The fact that the veil was torn from the top down, some 60 feet from the floor (where humans could not reach it), shows that God was the One that caused the veil to be torn.

The curtain was torn for you and I through Jesus death. Hebrews 10: 19-20 reads; *"Therefore, brothers and sisters, since we have confidence to enter the Most Holy Place by the blood of Jesus, 20 by a new and living way opened for us through the curtain, that is, his body"*. (NIV)

It took the mighty hand of God Himself to tear it supernaturally, and this tearing, which represents the removal of the separation between God and Man, could not be done by humans. He is the initiator of the veil being rent. He is the cause of the tearing. Jesus Christ, is the reason it was torn. It had to be done by God alone, and that's the point. No one can remove our separation from God but God Himself.

1John 2:2 says that *"He [Jesus] is the atoning sacrifice for our sins, and not only for ours but also for the sins of the whole world."* (NIV). Since Jesus' death atoned for our sins, Jesus' sacrifice allowed for the veil to be torn, and thus, the separation between God and Man was removed.

"Jesus' Death on the Cross dealt with the issue of sin once and for all".

It is no coincidence that the Temple sacrifices by Jewish Christians ceased that year and for the years to follow until eternity. Why? The sacrifices were stopped because of Jesus' offering of Himself. The temple priests did not accept Jesus' sacrifice in place of the animal sacrifices but believers in Him did.

The Book of Hebrews was written specifically to Jewish Christians, but the applications for us are the same. Hebrews 10 reveals that no other sacrifices were given, at least by the Jewish Christians. Luke's account of the birth and early history of the church in the Book of Acts never mentions any of the Christians continuing ritual sacrifices. They understood that the veil had been removed by Jesus' offering on the cross. Therefore, there was no further need to provide sacrifices, even at Passover or on the Day of Atonement.

Above all, the tearing of the veil at the exact time as Jesus death dramatically symbolized that His sacrifice, the shedding of His own blood, was enough atonement for all sins (past, present, and future). The way into the Holy of Holies was open for all people for all time, both Jew and Gentile, believers and unbelievers, pastor or that shameful sinner. Why? Because God moved out of that place (the physical Temple) into a living righteous Temple: YOU.

Never again to dwell in a Temple made with hands as seen in (Acts 17:24).

You don't go to church to meet
God's presence as a believer,
You carry God's presence to Church.

Praise God!! You and I are the mobile Temple of the presence of God. The presence of God is not in your church altar; the presence of God lives inside of you. You don't go to church to meet the presence of God; you carry the presence of God to church. You don't worship or sing to bring His presence down; His presence is already in you. Live with this audacious mindset.

The presence of God is no longer living in the Ark of the Covenant. We have a new covenant. A better and higher covenant. A covenant between God and Himself. The old covenant was between God and Man, but Mankind doesn't have the wherewithal to keep her own side of the agreement.

The old covenant was only for the chosen ones (the Israelites). The new covenant is for all, Jews or Gentiles. The old covenant needed Man's ability to keep the law, the new covenant needs Man to just believe in the finished work of Christ Jesus.

CHAPTER 3

IT IS FINISHED

The Significance of Jesus' Last Words.

The Bible says in John 19:30, *"When he had received the drink, Jesus said, 'It is finished.' With that, he bowed his head and gave up his spirit."* (NIV). In Mark 15:37 we read, *"With a loud cry, Jesus breathed his last."* (NIV). According to Bible scholars, this "loud cry" may have been those very last words that John records: "It is finished."

He spoke it out loud. He declared it for all to hear. He uttered a loud cry to His Father in heaven for the whole world to know, and for every evil force to have to flee. For Christ's work on the cross was complete.

Done.

Accomplished.

Paid in full.

Last words have power and, often, deep meaning and significance. If, like me, any of you have ever been at the side of a precious friend or family member who was whispering final words in their last moments here on earth, you know the incredible heart connection they hold for you.

We often find ourselves clinging to those words as we think about a loved one who has passed away. We treasure what they said, and we remember...There's no doubt that Jesus knew what His last words needed to be here in this life. He knew the power those final words would have for generations to come. And He had great purpose in them, which still breathe such life and meaning for our lives today.

"It is finished," one of Jesus' most important statements, is translated from the single Greek word *tetelestai.* The grammatical structure of the Greek word, perfect passive indicative, is very important.

It is finished:
A public declaration of the
believer's redemption.

The perfect tense indicates that the progress of an action has been completed and the result of that action is ongoing and with full effect. The passive voice indicates that the subject of the sentence is being acted upon in the indicative mode. Often, it was used in an accounting term, indicating that a debt was paid. What is unique about the way it was written is that the tense of the word indicates both the point in time it was complete and that it would also continue to be complete or finished.

Jesus became the final and ultimate sacrifice for our sin. This is the essence of what Christ came to do. He came to *finish* God's work of salvation in us. He came to *pay it in full*, the entire penalty or debt for our sins. He's still at work in our world today, in powerful ways.

While this may sound like more of a grammar lesson than most readers care for, this information is very important for understanding the significance of Jesus' words. Allow me to break it down.

What Did Jesus Finish?

Let's begin by identifying what the "it" is. What did Jesus finish? Jesus gives us the answer throughout the gospels, and the New Testament writers give us the answer throughout the Epistles. Let's look at these Scriptures below. There are lots of them though!! Matthew 5:17 reads; *"Do not think that I have come to abolish the Law or the Prophets; I have not come to abolish them but to fulfill them".*

Jesus obeyed the Father by being the perfect fulfillment of the Law of God and the prophecies regarding the Messiah. Jesus finished the work given to Him by His Father. *"Do not think that I have come to bring peace to the earth. I have not come to bring peace, but a sword. For I have come to set a man against his father, and a daughter against her mother, and a daughter-in-law against her mother-in-law. And a person's enemies will be those of his own household". Matthew 10:34-36 (ESV)*

Jesus did not come to preach a message of coexistence, tolerance, or ecumenism. Jesus made it clear that you are either with the One True God or against Him. Such truth was and is today the most divisive message the world has ever known. Jesus finished the work given to Him by His Father.

John 5:43 (ESV) reads, *I have come in my Father's name, and you do not receive me. If another comes in his own name, you will receive him.*

John 6:38 (ESV) reads, *For I have come down from heaven, not to do my own will but the will of him who sent me.*

Jesus came in the name of the only true God and to perfectly do His will. Jesus finished the work given to Him by His Father. He said, *"If I am not doing the works of my Father, then do not believe me; but if I do them, even though you do not believe me, believe the works, that you may know and understand that the Father is in me and I am in the Father". John 10:37-38 (ESV)*

Jesus came to do the works of His Father perfectly so people could understand that He and the Father were one (John 10:30). Jesus finished the work given to Him by His Father. Jesus came as the light of the world, giving fallen mankind the opportunity to move from utter darkness into His marvelous light. He came to save people. Jesus finished the work given to Him by His Father:

Then Pilate said to him, "So you are a king?" Jesus answered, "You say that I am a king. For this purpose, I was born and for this purpose I have come into the world — to bear witness to the truth. Everyone who is of the truth listens to my voice." John 18:37 (ESV)

Jesus also came as fully God and fully Man to be the incarnation of the Truth of God. Romans 3:21-25a (ESV) reads: *"But now the righteousness of God has been manifested apart from the law, although the Law and the Prophets bear witness to it— the righteousness of God through faith in Jesus Christ for all who believe. For there is no distinction: for all have sinned and fall short of the glory of God, and are justified by his grace as a gift, through the redemption that is in Christ Jesus, whom God put forward as a propitiation by his blood, to be received by faith".*

This was to show God's righteousness, because in His divine forbearance He had passed over former sins. It was to show His righteousness at the present time, so that He might be just and the Justifier of the one who has faith in Jesus. Jesus came to make reconciliation between God and Man possible.

Jesus came to die for and to purify His bride the "Church". Ephesians 5:25-27 (ESV) reads, *"Husbands, love your wives, as Christ loved the church and gave himself up for her, that he might sanctify her, having cleansed her by the washing of water with the word, so that he might present the church to himself in splendor, without spot or wrinkle or any such thing, that she might be holy and without blemish".*

Jesus came to glorify His Father through His life, death, and resurrection: Philippians 2:5-11 (ESV) reads, *"Have this mind among yourselves, which is yours in Christ Jesus, who, though he was in the form of God, did not count equality with God a thing to be grasped, but emptied himself, by taking the form of a servant, being born in the likeness of men. And being found in human form, he humbled himself by becoming obedient to the point of death, even death on a cross. Therefore God has highly exalted him and bestowed on him the name that is above every name, so that at the name of Jesus every knee should bow, in heaven and on earth and under the earth, and every tongue confess that Jesus Christ is Lord, to the glory of God the Father"*

Jesus came to make a way, the only way, for people to find mercy, grace, and help in time of need: Hebrews 4:14-16 (ESV) reads, *"Since then we have a great high priest who has passed through the heavens, Jesus, the Son of God, let us hold fast our confession. For we do not have a high priest who is unable to sympathize with our weaknesses, but one who in every respect has been tempted as we are, yet without sin. Let us then with confidence draw near to the throne of grace, that we may receive mercy and find grace to help in time of need".*

Jesus Declared His Work Finished!

Having identified the "it" (the work God the Father had given God the Son to accomplish on earth), let's look at what Jesus meant when He cried out that He had finished the work. As I mentioned earlier in this chapter, understanding the structure of the sentence in the Greek text helps us grasp the full weight of Christ's forever-memorable words.

What Jesus did through His perfect earthly existence, sacrificial death, and glorious resurrection fully completed the work the Father had given Him to do. Not only did He complete His salvation work, but His accomplishment is fully efficacious today and will be forevermore.

There is nothing more to add--nothing more to be done by God, Man, or religious institutions. The undeniable, factual, historic, and eternal work of Jesus Christ has been completed and will forever remain completed. Therefore, *It. Is. Finished!*

Jesus finished the work given to Him by His Father, which culminated at the cross. At the cross, the gavel of the Supreme Judge of the Universe crashed upon His mighty bench when God the Father p crush His Son and poured the full cup of the wrath of sin upon His innocent Son.

At the cross, the Great Exchange took place (2 Corinthians 5:21; Colossians 2:13-15). The eternal debt owed for the sin of mankind was paid in full. God the Father looked upon His perfect, precious, and priceless Son as if He had lived the filthy, detestable, sin-stained lives of fallen mankind.

And those who receive Jesus Christ as their Lord and Savior, God the Father looks upon as if they had lived His Son's perfect, precious, and priceless life. At the cross, God kept His promise to crush Satan's head through the bruising of His Son. The power of sin and death was vanquished once and for all time. Jesus Christ's finished work on the cross forever made man's work to appease God, to please God, and to be reconciled to God impotent and blasphemous.

The sin debt you and I owe to God was and is paid in full by our Lord and Savior, our Master and King, Jesus Christ when He shed His innocent blood on the cross on our behalf! It's FINISHED!

Implications of Tetelestai

The implications of Jesus' words on the cross are eternally positive for those who receive Jesus Christ as Lord and Savior--by the grace of God alone, through faith alone in Jesus Christ. However, the implications of Jesus' words on the cross are eternally negative for any organization or individual who seeks to add to, detract from, or replace not only Jesus' words on the cross, but also the work He accomplished to the glory of God the Father.

Every man-made religion and each of their faithful adherents stands right now in the crosshairs of God's wrath. John 3:34-36 reads: *"For he whom God has sent utters the words of God, for he gives the Spirit without measure. The Father loves the Son and has given all things into his hand. Whoever believes in the Son has eternal life; whoever does not obey the Son shall not see life, but the wrath of God remains on him. "* (ESV).

Roman Catholicism denies the efficacy of Jesus' finished work on the cross through the practice and observance of the mass and the sharing of the glory of Jesus Christ with his earthly Mother.

Jehovah's Witnesses deny the efficacy of Jesus' finished work on the cross by denying Christ died on the cross and by insisting one must be a member of the Watchtower Society and obey the Law of God to receive their brand of salvation.

Mormonism denies the efficacy of Jesus' finished work on the cross by adding their perceived righteousness and works to their salvation process. According to the Book of Mormon, salvation is by grace, plus works. It states in 2 Nephi 25:23, *"For we labor diligently to write, to persuade our children, and also our brethren, to believe in Christ, and to be reconciled to God; for we know that it is by grace that we are saved, after all we can do. "*

Islam denies the efficacy of Jesus' finished work on the cross by seeing Jesus as nothing more than a prophet, second to their own prophet Muhammad. They also believe it was Judas (a treacherous convert), not Jesus, who died on the cross.

Also, even among the Pentecostal community, many clerics and religious pundits still teach that Jesus is not the only way to the God the Father. Some have preached that once saved is not saved forever. Some have also taught their large crowds that baptism is a requirement for salvation. This and many other false doctrines make the work of Christ incomplete.

But the implications of Jesus' words on the cross extend beyond false doctrines and teachings. Some churches deny the efficacy of Jesus' finished work on the cross by insisting Jesus and the gospel need the help of man's innovation and perceived ability to make the gospel more palatable. This is demonstrated through gimmicks, sales pitches, bait, and switch tactics, and playing to the primal desires of health, wealth, prosperity, ease, comfort, and happiness.

Some churches deny the efficacy of Jesus' finished work on the cross by spending time and resources wooing the unsaved to the "Christian Club" instead of presenting faith in the Lord Jesus Christ finished works on the cross as the only central message from the pulpit. When Jesus said, "It is finished," He meant it. He meant what He said. He really meant it. For any group or any individual to add or detract from Christ's words or finished work, regardless of the religious stripes they wear, is the height of arrogance and the depth of depravity.

At the Cross,
the Wages of Sin was paid in Full.

It is finished. That is, the counsel and commandment of His Father concerning his sufferings were now fulfilled; it was a determinate counsel, and He took care to see every iota and tittle of it exactly answered. He had said, when He was suffering, "It is finished." That is, all the types and prophecies of the Old Testament, which pointed at the sufferings of the Messiah, were accomplished, and answered.

It is finished. The ceremonial law is abolished, and an end put to its obligation. The substance is now come, and all the shadows are done away with. The veil is rent; the wall of partition is taken down, even the law of commandments contained in ordinances. The Mosaic economy was dissolved to make way for a better hope. It is finished. Sin is finished and an end made of transgression by the bringing in of an everlasting righteousness. The Lamb of God was sacrificed to take away the sin of the world, and it is done. Hebrews 9:26 reads, *"Father, thy will be done"*, and now He saith with pleasure, it is done.

Usage of Tetelestai

There were several ways the word *tetelestai* was used in Greco-Roman culture—all of them illustrative of Jesus' finished work on the cross. Here are some examples. An artist might have said *Tetelestai*! when he finished a painting in order to announce, "the picture is perfect." Jesus, the Master Artisan, declared from the cross that the picture of salvation He had drawn from eternity past was always perfect but now complete. It is finished!

A servant might have confidently said *Tetelestai*! when asked by his master if the work he had been assigned to do was complete. The servant would say, "Yes, master. I have finished the work." Jesus, the Suffering Servant, completed the work His Father had given Him. It is finished!

A judge might have said *Tetelestai*! when he conferred a sentence or when issuing a ruling that a sentence had been completed. The judge would say, "Justice has been served." There is only one Lawgiver and Judge--only One who can save and destroy. And as the Father turned His back on His Son, the Father was well pleased. It pleased the Father to crush His Son. It is finished!

A priest might have said *Tetelestai*! when he recognized an unblemished and acceptable sacrifice for God. The priest would announce to the person offering the sacrifice that the offering was acceptable according to the law of God.

A merchant might have said *Tetelestai*! after stamping a bill "the debt has been paid." The Christian's debt has been paid in full by the propitiation of Jesus Christ. By Jesus paying the Christian's sin debt in full, (Colossians 2:13-15, ESV) reads, *"When you were dead in your transgressions and the uncircumcision of your flesh, God made us alive together with him, having forgiven us all our trespasses, by canceling the record of debt that stood against us with its legal demands. This he set aside, nailing it to the cross. He disarmed the rulers and authorities and put them to open shame, by triumphing over them in him."* It is finished!

A soldier might have said *Tetelestai*! as a battle cry toward a vanquished foe. The soldier would yell, "You are finished!" Jesus' cry on the cross was not a cry of despair or defeat. Oh, no. When Jesus cried with a loud voice, He was declaring victory over the enemy-Satan, sin, and death. It is finished!

The Artist had the last word as to the meaning of the painting—not the art critic. The Servant knew if the work in the house had been completed and approved by the Master—not the stranger who entered the house. The Judge determined the sentence, its execution, and its satisfaction, not the convicted criminal. The Priest determined if a sacrifice would be acceptable to God, not the penitent. The Merchant determined if a debt was paid, not the debtor. The Victorious Warrior determined the future of his combatant, not the defeated enemy.

Jesus Christ is the Artisan, the Servant, the Judge, the Priest, the Merchant, and the Victor. You are not. Your religion is not. Your intellect is not. Therefore, repent of any false ideologies that add works to Christ's finished work. Repent of any arrogant notions through manmade philosophies of ministry, which would presume to finish the work that Christ has already finished.

CHAPTER 4

THE SIN NATURE

For a long time, I was taught and made to believe that sin is each of the daily mistakes I make in my life as a believer. I was taught that sin is the lies, stealing, fornication, and all the weakness that my flesh falls for. But scripturally, this is not true. All the above are the products of the sin nature. Sin is first a noun and then a verb.

Sin is a nature (noun), and that is the nature of Satan. When the Bible addresses sin, most of the time it referred to sin as a noun, not as a verb. Few times in the Bible is the word sin used as a verb. Ok, calm down, we have a lot to talk about. Just keep reading.

Sin is a nature.
Jesus dealt with that nature through His death.

When the Bible refers to sin as a noun, it is describing the nature of Satan. When the Bible refers to sin as a verb, it is referring to the insignificant aspect, which is the behavior or actions that portray the noun sin, which is the nature. When Adam and Eve disobeyed God in the garden, they took up that nature. They gave up the nature of God in them and invited the sin nature into their lives.

Sin as a verb refers to things like lies, fornication, stealing – every behavior that doesn't represent Christ in you. But, it's important to note that sin as a verb is not what God was addressing in the perfect plan of salvation. God's interest was for Man to get rid of sin as a nature (noun) because that is the determining factor for whether a person receives eternal life.

Man is a tripartite being. He is a spirit, he has a soul, and lives in a body. In theology, this is known as trichotomy. How do we know about these three parts? Because we have been given this knowledge all through the Bible. The apostle Paul also revealed this fact in 1 Thessalonians 5:23: *"Now may the God of peace Himself sanctify you entirely; and may your spirit and soul and body be preserved complete, without blame at the coming of our Lord Jesus Christ." (NASB).*

Man is a spirit like his Creator God. He has a soul, which is the animate life: the seat of the sense, desires, affections, and appetite. The soul acts as a link between the material body and the spiritual sphere. Let's look at the scriptural references to this in the Bible.

According to the Bible, mankind is distinct from the rest of creation, including the animals. As I stated above, Man is made up of physical material (the body) which can be seen and touched. But he is also made up of immaterial, intangible aspects. These include the soul, spirit, intellect, will, emotions, conscience, and so forth. These immaterial characteristics exist beyond the physical lifespan of the human body and are therefore eternal. These immaterial aspects -- the spirit, soul, heart, conscience, mind, and emotions -- make up the whole personality. The Bible makes it clear that the soul and spirit are the primary immaterial aspects of humanity, while the body is the physical container that holds them on this earth.

The Body (Greek word "soma')

The body is the entire material or physical structure of a human being, the physical part of a person. The Apostle Paul, writing to the Romans again connects the body, the mind (soul), and the spirit. *"Therefore, I urge you, brethren, by the mercies of God, to present your bodies a living and holy sacrifice, acceptable to God, which is your spiritual service of worship. And do not be conformed to this world, but be transformed by the renewing of your mind, so that you may prove what the will of God is, that which is good and acceptable and perfect. Romans 12:1-2 (NASB).*

The Soul (Greek, psyche)

Genesis 2:7 tells us that Man was created as a "living soul." The soul consists of the mind (which includes the conscience), the will, and the emotions. The soul and the spirit are mysteriously tied together and make up what the Scriptures call the "heart."

The writer of Proverbs declares, *"Watch over your heart with all diligence, for from it flow the springs of life."* (Proverbs 4:23, NASB). We see here that the "heart" is central to our emotions and will. *"But a natural (psuchikos*

-- soulish) man does not accept the things of the Spirit of God, for they are foolishness to him; and he cannot understand them, because they are spiritually appraised." 1 Corinthians 2:14 (NASB)

Paul, looking intently at the Council, said, "Brethren, I have lived my life with a perfectly good conscience before God up to this day." Acts 23:1 (NASB)

The Spirit (Greek, pneuma)

In Numbers 16:22, Moses and Aaron, "...fell upon their faces and said, 'O God, God of the spirits of all flesh, when one man sins, will You be angry with the entire congregation?'" (NASB). They name God as the God of the spirits that are possessed by all humanity. Notice also that it mentions the flesh (body) of all mankind, connecting it with the spirit.

Another key verse that describes the separation between soul and spirit is Hebrews 4:12: "For the word of God is living and active and sharper than any two-edged sword, and piercing as far as the division of soul and spirit, of both joints and marrow, and able to judge the thoughts and intentions of the heart." (NASB). We see in this Scripture that the soul and spirit can be divided -- and that it is the Word of God that pierces our heart to bring the division of soul and spirit, something that only God can do.

Now, having laid down this foundation, let's continue the topic of sin as a nature. Imagine a cherry tree in your mind. The nature of sin we are talking about here is the root of the tree, while the branches and trunk are the behaviors of sin, or the "sin" as a verb.

Through His death on the cross, Jesus took away the root of sin which is the nature of sin. Now the question I would like to ask you is this: can a tree survive when the roots are destroyed? The answer is NO. Why? Because it will have no means of getting important nutrients from the soil to survive. It will have no anchor to the earth. When Jesus died, He destroyed the nature of sin in you. He took that nature away. He took that old root and gave you a new nature, the nature of righteousness.

Understanding Romans 6:1-2

"What shall we say then? Shall we continue in sin, that grace may increase? The answer to this scripture is not even verse 2 but the same verse 1. The sin mentioned in this verse is a NOUN. This is the nature of sin from Adam. Notice it didn't say "shall we continue to sin?" It said, "shall we continue in sin?"

The Bible says in 2 Corinthians 5:17 *"if any man be in Christ, he is a new creature. "*. Do you notice the use of the words "in Christ" and "in sin"? This means you cannot continue in sin once you are in Christ. It's just an impossible situation. That old man is dead to that sin nature as used in Romans 6 verse 2. You are alive in Christ and have the righteous nature of Christ in you.

Sin as a verb doesn't take one to Hell.
Unbelief in the finished work of Christ Does.

You can either be in sin or be in Christ. There are no two ways about it. Once you are in Christ, you can never go back to being in sin. Because as far as sin is concerned, you are dead to it. Most people will argue, "But how come you are still committing sin?" Now, like I said earlier, there is sin as a noun, which is the nature, and sin (acts) as a verb.

When you were born again, the nature of sin (Noun) died, and a new nature, which is the life of Christ, was born. You now live the life of Christ. But know that this happened in your spirit man, not in your five senses, so you don't feel anything, neither do you see any changes in your flesh.

Your thoughts are the same, but your spirit is 100% perfect as Jesus is. Jesus said that as He is in Heaven, so are you here on Earth. He didn't say so you will be. It's not a process. It happened the moment you were born again. But you need to renew your mind as apostle Paul instructed in Romans 12, so you can be the beginning to see the new man in you manifest in your physical body since the old man left this old mindset with you.

Salvation doesn't dispose carnal behaviors instantly, but the consistent hearing of the undiluted principles of the Word of God does. Receiving Jesus into your life doesn't automatically stop you from lying, fornicating, etc. It was your spirit that was transformed, not your mind of flesh.

But as you keep growing in the Lord and hearing the Word of God and putting it into practice you, you will gradually begin taking control of the lust of the flesh through the help of the Holy Spirit in you. That is one purpose of the Holy Spirit in you, to help you overcome the lust of the flesh.

It's not something you can do on your own. It is a process. No condemnation, no guilt. You will still find yourself at different points in your life, perhaps daily, doing those things you say you won't do. It's fine. Don't feel guilty or ashamed. We are all humans. Nobody is perfect by his/her works. Our flesh is weak, and we all have weakness that we are dealing with daily. The good news is you are saved and righteous in the eyes of God. You have the gentle sweet help of the Holy Spirit as you grow into full maturity in Christ Jesus. The next chapter is even more appetizing!!

CHAPTER 5

THE FIVE CONTENTS OF THE PACKAGE OF REDEMPTION

One beautiful thing about your new life in Christ is that it's complete. There is no addition or subtraction, everything was included. There are five contents that come with your redemption, and I will share them with you. I would like you to have them at the tip of your finger, memorize them, speak them loud to yourself in your house, your bathroom, or when driving.

Why is it important to know and be conscious of this package of redemption? Because the ignorance of it is the only avenue through which Satan can mess with your mind. Ignorance of these five contents of the package of redemption will cause you to live in condemnation, guilt and acting like a slave or servant, whereas you have been made a son/daughter in the kingdom.

Friend, if you become aware of the benefits that came with your redemption, you will never fall victim to false prophets or be tossed around by every wind of doctrine just as the Scriptures cautioned us about. (See Ephesians 4:14).

The day you confessed Jesus as your Lord and Savior, beloved, was the same day you received this delivery from Jesus Christ.

The delivery of the package of redemption was faster than next day air delivery by FedEx, USPS, or UPS. The delivery of this package is faster than Amazon Prime shipping, and guess what? The contents of the package of redemption are all eternal and forever.

There is no expiration date, when you received it, the Manufacturer in the person of Jesus Christ who shipped it to you, has guaranteed that it has a life time warranty and beyond that, it has an eternal warranty. Nothing can destroy this. Nothing can take it away from you. It can't be stolen. There is nothing that you can do to warrant Jesus to take it back from you. Hallelujah!!!!

What are these five Contents of the packages of Redemption?

Before we consider the package of redemption, let's look at the dictionary meaning of redemption. According to the Oxford dictionary, redemption is defined as "the action of regaining or gaining possession of something in exchange for payment or clearing a debt." It also defines it as "the action of saving or being saved from sin, error or evil." Redemption is also the Greek word *exagora*, meaning buying, repurchase, ransom, take over, or buyout. Okay, now let's go on.

Have you bought a set of products before online or in a store and went home to open the package? Immediately you start checking to see if all the expected contents, as advertised on the labels, are intact and in good shape. Well let me share a short experience I had. Christmas 2018, a friend sent me an awfully expensive Christmas gift. It was a five-piece cooking set, all the way from Japan...

When the package was shipped, my friend texted, "Hello obi, I sent you a package, and you should receive it in two days' time. Please when you do open the package check for any dents, missing parts. If you find any, do let me know so it can be returned because the package comes with 20 years manufacturer warranty and even shipping insurance in case the package goes missing or damaged during handling by the shipping company."

When my package was delivered by DHL, I ran with it into the kitchen and began opening it. First was a big well-designed pot; second was a nice colorful big cooking spoon. There was also a medium size pot, a big stainless-steel bowl with a gold colored handle, and finally a set of cutleries.

I was so excited about my Christmas gift, but that happiness was cut short a little bit because, as I went through the individual details of the content in the package, I discovered that two items in the cutlery set were missing. I received my package in good shape, but a few items were missing but later sent to me.

I have good news for you. Your redemption package came complete. You received all the gifts inside of it. There are some Christians who feel like all they got from Christ's death was redemption and that there are still some things lacking in their Christian life which they cannot receive until after death. Folks, this is a mindset created by false doctrines of legalism and ignorance of the finished works of Jesus.

CONTENT #1: FORGIVENESS OF SIN

Forgiveness of sins is one of the great themes of the Bible. There is so much that Scripture says about it that it would take volumes of books to adequately deal with the subject. Suffice it to say that the blood of Jesus is what provided us with forgiveness of sins. That sacrifice was so great that it outweighed all our sins. It covered all the sins of the world – past, present, and future.

Like my cooking set, forgiveness of sin is one of the contents in the redemption package you received through Jesus Christ the day you became born again. Like I explained to you in previous chapters, forgiveness of sins is not something you asked for. It was a gift contained in your redemption package.

You did not earn it, neither was it given to you because you prayed and fasted in tears. The day you confessed and believed Jesus as your Lord and Savior, you received the forgiveness for all your sins. Most Christians understand the concept that the sins they committed before they professed faith in Christ are forgiven at salvation but believe that any sins committed after that time are not forgiven until they repent and ask for forgiveness. This is not the case.

All our sins – past, present, and future – were forgiven through the one offering of Jesus. If God can't forgive future sins, then none of us can be saved because Jesus only died once, nearly 2,000 years ago, before we had committed any sins. All our sins have been forgiven.

The forgiveness of our sins is not the ultimate goal of our salvation. It is just a necessary step. The real goal of salvation is relationship with the Father, and sin is a barrier to that relationship. So, it had to be dealt with, and it was, through the blood of our Lord Jesus Christ. But those who stop with the forgiveness of sins and don't go on into eternal life are missing the heart of salvation.

Our sins have been forgiven so that we may enter into intimacy with the Lord. It is through the riches of God's grace that we have received forgiveness for our sins. There is nothing we can do to obtain forgiveness except humble ourselves and receive forgiveness as a gift through faith in Christ.

Stop Praying for the Forgiveness of Sin as a Believer

Praying and asking God for the forgiveness of sin as a born-again believer is on it's own a sin. Why? Because you are walking in unbelief. I'm going to begin this by dropping a bomb: Sin is no longer an issue with God; we are redeemed! With that statement, you are either rejoicing, shocked, or confused. That is one radical statement, but one I believe I can back up by the Word of God.

The message most people hear says that sin breaks your relationship or fellowship with God. The strictest message says that you lose your salvation ("backslide") every time you sin, until it's confessed. Others believe your eternal salvation is still secure, but you lose fellowship, can't get your prayers answered, or can't be used by God if you sin. That's not good news, since all of us sin (Romans 3:23 and 1 John 1:8).

Christians usually cope by trying to keep every sin confessed. Let me just put this bluntly: That's impossible! The Bible says that whatever is not of faith is sin (Romans 14:23). Do we always walk in faith? James 4:17 reveals that sin isn't only doing things that are wrong, but it's not doing what we know is right. Would any claim they are loving God and others as they know they should?

By these definitions, we all sin through the weakness of our flesh. It's impossible to keep every sin confessed. Even if it were possible, that puts the burden of salvation on our backs. There wouldn't be any peace or rest in our relationship with the Lord if that's the way it worked. (*See* Romans 5:1).

Most people, including Christians, see the forgiveness of sins as something that God can do, and continues to do, but not as something He has completed. From that comes the false concept that we must constantly confess our sins, which makes and keeps us sin conscious.

The New Testament presents the forgiveness of sins as something that is already accomplished and that the effect of this redemption is that we are not even to be conscious of sin (Hebrews 10:1-2). Ask yourself, what produced the forgiveness of sins and when did that happen? Jesus was the Lamb of God that took away the sins of the world as recorded in John 1:29. It was through the shedding of Jesus' blood that you received redemption, which is the forgiveness of your sins. (Ephesians 1:7 and Colossians 1:14).

When did Jesus die and shed His blood for our sins? About 2,000 years ago. He will never die again (Romans 6:9-10). He dealt with the sins of the whole human race once, for all time (Hebrews 9:25-28 and 10:10-14). Jesus' sacrifice for our sins is already an accomplished work.

We don't have to ask Jesus to forgive our sins; He's already done it. Paul didn't tell the Philippian jailor to ask Jesus to forgive him; Paul told him to believe on what Jesus had already done and he would be saved. (See Acts 16:31). We confess the Lord Jesus, not our sins, to receive this gift of salvation (Romans 10:9)

Does that mean everyone in the whole world is saved? Certainly not. We have to receive forgiveness by faith (Acts 26:18). The Lord has already forgiven everyone's sins (1 John 2:2). That's grace. But we must put faith in what God has already accomplished by grace to be saved (Ephesians 2:8).

Therefore, it's not a person's many sins that send him to hell; sin has already been paid for and forgiven. It's the singular sin of not believing on Jesus that sends a person to hell. It's his/her failure to accept what Jesus did that puts him into that place of eternal torment. John 16:8-9 reads, *"And when he is come, he will reprove the world of sin, and of righteousness, and of judgment: Of sin, because they believe not on me."*

The singular sin the Holy Spirit reproves us of is the sin of not believing on Jesus. That's it. That's not to say that the Holy Spirit will not show us that things we do are wrong. But He uses what we do to illustrate that we don't believe on Jesus. The Holy Spirit isn't nailing us every time we sin; He loves us back into faith and trust in Jesus. That's the whole picture with God.

What difference does it make in our lives whether we accept forgiveness as something that has already been accomplished? There is a huge difference! It gives us security and peace, knowing that God isn't mad at us and won't be mad at us. Our sins are already forgiven—and not just the past sins we committed before we were born again. All of our sins—past, present, and even future ones—are already forgiven.

Someone will say, "How can God forgive our sins before we commit them?" Well, you better pray that He can do that, because Jesus only died for our sins once, 2,000 years ago, before you committed any sin. If He can't forgive sins before you commit them, then you can't be saved. Hebrews 10:10-12, 14 declares, *"By the which will we are sanctified through the offering of the body of Jesus Christ once for all. And every priest standeth daily ministering and offering oftentimes the same sacrifices, which can never take away sins: But this man, after he had offered one sacrifice for sins forever, sat down on the right hand of God; ...For by one offering he hath perfected forever them that are sanctified."*

We have received eternal, not momentary redemption. (*See* Hebrews 9:12). One sacrifice was made for all sin forever, and we have been perfected forever. How can we read these scriptures and come to any other conclusion than that every sin—past, present, and future—was forgiven and our redemption is eternal?

If you have accepted the sacrifice of Jesus for your sins by faith, then your spirit is perfect (Hebrews 12:23)! Your spirit has been born again. A million years from now, your spirit will be identical to what it is right now, and it is identical to Jesus (See 1 Corinthians 6:17 and 1 John 4:17).

So, am I making light of sin or saying sin doesn't matter? No! Sin is a terrible thing, and it's an inroad for Satan into your life (Romans 6:16). I hate sin! I live a holier life than most people reading this. But I just value the blood and the atonement of Jesus above sin. His sacrifice was infinitely greater than all the past, present, and future transgressions of the entire human race. Jesus overpaid the debt we owed.

You might say, "What about 1 John 1:9?" Well, I'm glad you brought that up. First John 1:9 (KJV) says, *"If we confess our sins, [God] is faithful and just to forgive us our sins, and to cleanse us from all unrighteousness."*

We don't have to confess sin in order to be saved, to retain, or to maintain our salvation. If I believed that was so, I would kill every person who came forward for salvation. I might go to hell, but that's the only way they would ever get to heaven. We need to confess it, not for the purpose of becoming born again, but because when we sin, our flesh gets defiled. That gives Satan a legal right to function in our flesh (Romans 6:16).

The act of constantly asking for forgiveness of sins during prayer is foolishness and a sign of scriptural illiteracy.

Confessing we have sinned means we are coming back into agreement with God and out of agreement with the devil. That stops Satan from dominating us through that sin and draws the forgiveness and purity, which is already in our born-again spirits, out into our flesh.

Our born-again spirits are already eternally redeemed (Hebrews 9:12). The other two-thirds, your soul and body, have also been purchased by His blood, but their salvation has not yet taken place. However, God has made provision for this as well. As you grow in the knowledge of the person of Jesus, your body and mind is transformed.

"Romans 8:23 reads, *"And not only they, but ourselves also, which have the first fruits of the Spirit, even we ourselves groan within ourselves, waiting for the adoption, to wit, the redemption of our body*

Ephesians 1:14 reads, *"Which is the earnest of our inheritance until the redemption of the purchased possession, unto the praise of his glory."*

When redemption is complete in spirit, soul, and body, we will know God as we are known by Him (1 Corinthians 13:12). But until then, we can experience a renewed mind through His Word. And although we are waiting for the redemption of our bodies, we can receive healing while we live in our mortal bodies. God has made provision for both the soul and the body, even though their redemption has not yet been made manifest.

Unfortunately, most Christians are not taking advantage of these provisions. They have not renewed their minds, and they still don't understand that we are also redeemed from the curse of the Law (Galatians 3:13). The average New Testament believer is still trying to get God to respond to him/her based on performance. Why? Because they don't know that the performance covenant of the Old Testament Law is over. We are now under the New Testament ministry of grace and faith (2 Corinthians 3:7-8).

The Law was given to convict people of their self-righteousness so they could see their need for a savior. Praise God, we are now no longer under the Law. First Timothy 1:9 says that the Law is not made for a righteous man. And who is righteous? Any person who is born again

(2 Corinthians 5:21). Hebrews 7:12,18 reads, *"For the priesthood being changed, there is made of necessity a change also of the law. ...For there is verily a disannulling of the commandment going before for the weakness and unprofitable thereof."*

What a radical statement! A disannulling! The word disannulling literally means cancellation, to make null and void. The Old Testament Law has been nullified, canceled, done away with. The Law was weak and unprofitable. It was only a stop-gap measure until Jesus (Galatians 3:23-25).

Ephesians 1:3-5 says, *"[He] hath blessed us with all spiritual blessings...hath chosen us...Having predestined us unto the adoption of children."* In the Greek, "hath" is an aorist tense, which means it is a done deal—it's an accomplished fact. So how blessed is all spiritual blessings? Verse 6 says that we have been accepted in the beloved. Really, that is a super understatement.

The Greek word that is used for "accepted" is only used twice in the New Testament. The other place is in Luke where the Angel Gabriel appeared unto Mary. Gabriel said, *"Hail thou that are highly favored, the Lord is with thee."* (Luke 1:28). The Greek word for "highly favored" is the only other time that this word was used. When Paul says in Ephesians that we are accepted in the beloved, he is saying God has made us highly favored. Mary hasn't got anything on a born-again believer. Every one of us is accepted, chosen, and highly favored. It's all part of redemption.

Understanding redemption, the complete forgiveness of your sins, is foundational to understanding the New Covenant and how God deals with you today. If you're born again and still asking questions like these: "Can I lose my salvation?" or "If I die with unconfessed sin, will I go to heaven?" or "Does God answer the prayers of someone who still sins?" then you do not understand redemption. Redemption is very practical, and your understanding of it will determine what you are able to receive from God, not just in eternity, but here and now.

Forgiveness Sins Before and After The Cross

Apostle Paul wrote to the Colossians Church as recorded in Colossians 1: 14 *"In whom we have redemption through his blood, even the forgiveness of sins".*

People received forgiveness of sins before the coming of Jesus Christ. During the life of Christ on earth, he forgave sins and people also were forgiven. After the cross of Christ, people still receive forgiveness. Though they are all forgiveness, the nature or character of the forgiveness differs.

Before the cross and under the Law of Moses, forgiveness of sin was possible by following the requirement in the law for specific sins committed. Almost all sins were atoned for by the sacrifice of a lamb and some of the sins too, the offender would have to be removed from among people or stoned to death, (John 8: 4- 5). Sin was not totally removed and this necessitated yearly confessions or reminders and offerings of animals like I said early on.

Forgiveness was obtained on the condition of repentance. Forgiveness was also for sins already committed. Any new sin committed after forgiveness is treated as a new case, (John 5: 14). Before the cross, a man had to forgive his neighbor before God could also forgive him or even answer his prayers, (Matthew 6: 14- 15).

After the cross, that is, after the death, burial and resurrection of Jesus Christ, forgiveness is now based solely on the shed blood of Jesus Christ and it is the forgiveness of all sins. No one is supposed to be killed or stoned for any sin. All sins have been paid for by Christ. After the cross forgiveness is granted once when a person believes the gospel of Christ.

This forgiveness covers all past, present and future sins of the believer. This implies that even when a man sins after being forgiven in Christ, his sin is not counted against him. He is only expected to change his ways, that is repent from the wrong act, but his repentance does not in any way become the basis for which he is forgiven. No condition is attached to our forgiveness in Christ.

After the cross, we are expected to forgive others of their sins but forgiving others does not become the condition for our forgiveness in Christ, (Hebrews 10: 1- 18). Since God has already forgiven the man in Christ based on the one- time sacrifice of Jesus, (1John 2: 1- 2, 1John 2: 12), our forgiveness is therefore not a prayer topic.

Like I have explained several times in this book, we don't pray to be forgiven. We believe we have been forgiven all our sin in Christ, (Colossians 2: 13). Forgiveness is, therefore, ours to take based on the knowledge of Jesus shed blood and not a request to make.

Forgiveness before the cross was selective, temporal, and conditional. Forgiveness after the cross is for all sins, it is eternal and unconditional for the man in Christ. As Christians, we have total, eternal and complete one-time forgiveness in Christ. This knowledge for the man who is born again with a new nature does not result in abuse of God's forgiveness but result in making him bold and confident in defeating the voice of the accuser and making him reign in life or righteousness, (Romans 5: 17).

Content #2: Eternal Life

Another important content in the package of redemption is eternal life. Wow!!! I'm so happy this was included in my redemption package. The subject of eternal life is still wrongly taught and poorly understood by many Christians today. To many, eternal life is seen as something out of this natural world. Some see eternal life as a reward after death.

Someone might say, "Eternal life is living forever." But that's not it. No one ceases to exist when they die. Everyone lives forever in either heaven or hell. "Well then, eternal life must be living forever in heaven instead of hell." That's not it either.

John 3:36 says, *"He that believeth on the Son hath everlasting life: and he that believeth not the Son shall not see life; but the wrath of God abided on him. "* Everlasting life is a present-tense possession. It's not something that begins when we get to heaven. There are several Scriptures that speak of everlasting life as something we possess in this life. (*See,* John 4:14; 5:24; 6:27, 40, 47).

So, the question remains, "What is everlasting life?" This is particularly important. John 3:16 says it was the reason that Jesus came. *"For God so loved the world, that he gave his only begotten Son, that whosoever believeth in him should not perish, but have everlasting life. ".*

Many people have mistakenly thought that the goal of salvation is the forgiveness of sin to avoid hell. That's not what John 3:16 is saying. Sure, not perishing in hell is an important part of what Jesus came to do. He accomplished that by paying the debt for all our sins – past, present, and even the ones we haven't committed yet.

If that's all there was to salvation, it's more than any of us deserve, and it would still be worth preaching. But salvation is much more than getting our sins forgiven so we can go to heaven instead of hell. Let me say it this way. If all you did was ask Jesus to forgive your sins so you wouldn't perish in hell, then you are missing out on eternal life. Sin was a barrier that stood between us and a holy God. It had to be removed. That's exactly what Jesus did, and He did it well.

Sin is no longer standing between God and Man (2 Corinthians 5:17). But to what does that entitle us? Sure, it entitles us to live forever with God in heaven. That's wonderful. But there are tremendous benefits right here, right now, on earth. Eternal life is one of those benefits. Jesus defined eternal life for us in John 17:3. *"And this is life eternal, that they might know thee the only true God, and Jesus Christ, whom thou hast sent."*. Eternal life is knowing God. You may be disappointed with that definition. You think you know God, and you still aren't satisfied. You want there to be something more.

The key lies in understanding what the Bible means by this word "know. It speaks of much more than just intellectual knowledge. It is in hundreds of Scriptures, like, *"Adam knew Eve his wife; and she conceived, and bare Cain."* (Genesis 4:1). Adam didn't just know Eve intellectually. That wouldn't produce children. He had an intimate, personal experience with her. This was speaking of a knowing between a man and a woman in the most intimate way possible.

Likewise, when Jesus said eternal life was knowing God, He was speaking of having an intimate, close, personal relationship with God. That's awesome! Many people believe Jesus died to forgive their sins, but they still don't have a close, personal, intimate relationship with their Father God. They think that is reserved for heaven. They are content to muddle through life singing songs about how, when we all get to heaven, what a day that will be.

That is not to take anything away from heaven, but we are supposed to have eternal life (close, intimate, personal relationship with God our Father and Jesus Christ His Son) right now. It's not "pie in the sky by and by" but rather "steak on your plate while you wait."

Jesus said in John 3:16 that God loved the world so much, He gave His only begotten Son so those who believed on Him wouldn't perish but would have everlasting life. If all you have done is believe on Jesus so you won't go to hell, then you are missing out on the everlasting life the Lord wants to have with you right now.

Why is this so misunderstood? It is because the church has changed the message of salvation. They have placed a period after the word "perish" in John 3:16. They have told the world that the reason God sent His Son to die for their sins was so they wouldn't perish, PERIOD. That excludes the true message of eternal life and intimate relationship with God as the goal of salvation.

Faith comes from hearing God's Word (Romans 10:17). If we don't hear that Jesus came to bring us back into intimate relationship with God, then we won't exercise faith for that, and we won't experience it. This describes the modern-day church to a tee. We have many people who have come to the Lord and received the forgiveness of their sins, but they are saved and stuck, just waiting for heaven so they can really start living. That is missing the main point of salvation.

If there was no afterlife, if there was no heaven or hell, John 3:16 reveals that Jesus would still have come and died for our sins so we could once again have an intimate relationship with Him and His Father right now, in this present evil world (Galatians 1:4). This was one of the main differences between the first-century church and our modern church. Those people knew God intimately. They had a relationship with the Lord that wasn't waiting to start in heaven but was working in them while they were still in this world.

They didn't have the advantages of radio, television, internet, or any other modern means of communication. They never even put a bumper sticker on a camel. Yet, these believers turned the known world upside down with the truths of the Gospel in just thirty years (Acts 17:6). They impacted their world much more than we are impacting our world today. Why? They had such a depth of relationship with a Living God that it was contagious.

In Rome, Christians knew their God so intimately that they sang His praises as they were burned at the stake. There are historical accounts of Nero the emperor sticking his fingers in his ears and saying, "Why must these Christians sing?"

They had much more than a doctrine and a hope. They had a present-tense relationship that allowed them to endure terrible atrocities with joy. There are historical accounts of Romans, when witnessing the joy of these Christians who were being martyred, jumping out of the stands and rushing to them. They knew they would be doomed to the same fate, but they willingly accepted death so they could know God in the same close, intimate, and personal way as these Christians.

Once you understand that true eternal life begins with a personal relationship with the Lord, it leads to a question: "How do I begin?" That's an important question with an important answer. Let me ask you this question. It's not intended to condemn you, but to enlighten you. How many people would die to have what you have? Is anyone envious of your relationship with the Lord? If not, then may I suggest to you that you aren't experiencing eternal life as the Bible describes it and as our Lord Jesus died to give you.

This isn't something for the select few. This is normal Christian living. In fact, if this isn't your experience, you aren't really living. This is what drove the Apostle Paul and all the early Christians (Philippians 3:10). It's still what drives victorious Christians today. It's all about personal relationship with a Person, not just some doctrine.

Content #3: Righteousness and Justification

Often in this book you will see the term righteousness and justification. This is one of the contents inside our redemption package. Like other contents, righteousness and justification are both gifts to us through Jesus Christ's death. The subject of righteousness cannot be overemphasized. It's at the heart of the benefit of the new creation reality.

One great attribute of Jesus Christ's righteousness which we received, is the fact that it takes away any room for pride or self-boosting since we all received it as a gift and not by the works of our deeds.

People who are self-righteous often despise others. No one can compare himself with God's perfect standard and feel good about himself. To trust in ourselves, we have to constantly compare ourselves to others. This breeds a critical attitude towards others that exalts self by debasing others.

No one can ever be righteous in the sight of God through his own righteousness. Our actions benefit us in relationships with people and prevent Satan from having an opportunity against us, but they cannot make us right (righteous) with God. We must trust in God and receive His gift of righteousness completely on the basis of faith in what Christ did for us. This is the truth that this parable is presenting.

Romans 5:17-19 reads, *For if by one man's offence death reigned by one; much more they which receive abundance of grace and of the gift of righteousness shall reign in life by one, Jesus Christ. Therefore as by the offence of one judgment came upon all men to condemnation; even so by the righteousness of one the free gift came upon all men unto justification of life. For as by one man's disobedience many were made sinners, so by the obedience of one shall many be made righteous.*

Most people are unaware that there are two kinds of righteousness. But only one type of righteousness is acceptable to God. One form of righteousness is our own righteousness. These are the acts of morality and holiness that we do in an attempt to fulfill the commands of the Old

Testament law. This is an imperfect righteousness because human nature is imperfect and incapable of fulfilling the law.

God's righteousness is not something that we do but something that we receive as a gift through faith in Christ. It's not possible to trust in our own righteousness and in God's righteousness. A person who believes that he must earn God's acceptance by his holy actions must not believe in God's righteousness, which is a gift. It has to be one or the other; we cannot mix the two. Righteousness is not what Jesus has done for us plus some minimum standard of holiness that we have to accomplish. God's righteousness is perfect. Accept this gift He offers to you.

Jesus Is Enough

Would God send His only Son to bear our sin, becoming sin itself, and then judge Him without mercy for that sin if His sacrifice wasn't enough? No! Yet, many Christians act as though it wasn't enough and continue to believe God is withholding His blessing because of their sin. It's time to renew your mind with the tuth.

Over the course of a few years, I have ministered to hundreds of people who just won't let the Bible get in the way of their theology. Religious traditions and widely accepted teachings have become the basis of their beliefs, rather than the Bible. The results are obvious: Their relationship with Christ is profiting them little, or at the very least less, than God intended.

These are people who have accepted Jesus as their Savior. Yet, they can't get healed; they're unhappy, depressed, fearful, and full of unbelief. That shouldn't be!

As you read, I encourage you to allow the Bible, God's Word, to get right in the middle of your theology.

Let me start by making this radical statement. If you're conscious of sin, then you truly don't understand the grace of your salvation through Jesus. It sounds radical, but it's true. That is totally different than the way most people think. I'm not saying this to hurt anybody, because I understand; I struggle with the same thing.

It's different than what most of us have been told. But this is what God's Word declares. In 2 Corinthians 5:19; *"To wit, that God was in Christ, reconciling the world unto himself, not imputing their trespasses unto them; and hath committed unto us the word of reconciliation"*. God is not imputing, or laying to our account, our sin.

Sin consciousness has been ground into us. Grace is not the way of the world. Your employer doesn't hire you by grace and promise to pay no matter what you do; they have expectations of performance. In marriage, spouses don't always love each other unconditionally. Even in most Christian families, children are either rewarded or punished based on their performance.

In this earth almost everything is based on performance, and because it is, it always forces us to focus on our weaknesses. That performance mentality then transfers into religion, where we're taught to focus on our sin. However, where God is concerned, it's just the opposite. In fact, sin isn't even an issue with God. Why? Because our sin is not being imputed, or charged, to our account. It's being charged to Jesus' account, and He already paid the bill.

I know a lot of churches that would throw me out of their pulpit for saying this, but it's what the Bible teaches.

It's time to let the Bible get in the way of wrong theology. Hebrews is one of my favorite books of the Bible. I wish I had space to put the whole book into context because it has a lot to say about how God dealt with sin. Hebrews 9:11-12 reads; *"But Christ being come an high priest of good things to come, by a greater and more perfect tabernacle, not made with hands, that is to say, not of this building; Neither by the blood of goats and calves, but by his own blood he entered in once into the holy place, having obtained eternal redemption for us"*.

If words mean anything, think about these words: Jesus entered in once! Do you know what once means in the Greek? It means once. It means He doesn't do it over and over again. Every time you sin, the Lord doesn't have to wait until you repent and then get that sin under the blood.

Most Christians believe that when you're born again, you get your sins forgiven up to that point. Then, every time you sin after becoming a Christian, you've got to run to the Lord with that sin and confess and repent, or you could be lost. If not lost and on your way to hell, then at the very least, God would not fellowship with you, and He certainly wouldn't answer your prayers.

Like I said before, if that were true, then everybody would be on their way to hell. There isn't a person on this earth who doesn't have either a known or an unknown unconfessed sin. Or, if sin just means the loss of relationship with God and unanswered prayers, then God wouldn't have a single person qualified to receive an answer to prayer or fellowship with Him. Was Jesus enough or not?

This is a huge issue. It's the reason many believe God isn't healing them or prospering them. They say out of one side of their mouths that He loves them and sacrificed His son Jesus, for their salvation, and then out of the other side, they say that He is still judging them for sin. This are incompatible! The scripture says, *"For if the blood of bulls and of goats, and the ashes of an heifer sprinkling the unclean, sanctifieth to the purifying of the flesh: How much more shall the blood of Christ, who through the eternal Spirit offered himself without spot to God, purge your conscience from dead works to serve the living God? And for this because he is the mediator of the new testament, that by means of death, for the redemption of the transgressions that were under the first testament, they which are called might receive the promise of eternal inheritance".* Hebrews 9:13-15

It isn't God who is condemning us when we sin but our own consciences. We haven't purged our consciences with the truth of what Jesus has done with sin. Satan knows that and is using it to condemn us and destroy our faith and confidence in God by reminding us we don't deserve God's blessing.

Praise God, He isn't giving you what you deserve; He is giving you what Jesus deserves. Jesus paid for sin one time, past, present, and even the sins you will commit in the future. How can that be, you ask? I don't know exactly, but let me tell you this, Jesus only died one time for our sins two thousand years ago, so you better hope He can forgive your sins before you commit them.

The scriptures declares in Hebrews 9:25-28a *"Nor yet that he should offer himself often, as the high priest entereth into the holy place every year with the blood of others; For then must he often have suffered since the foundation of the world: but now once in the end of the world hath he appeared to put away sin by the sacrifice of himself. And as it is appointed unto men once to die, but after this the judgment".* So, Christ was once offered to bear the sins of many

God knows the end from the beginning, and He knew all the sins of the whole world. Jesus paid for all those committed before His sacrifice and for all that had not yet been committed. He made the payment once, and it will never be made again. The price for sin, all sin, has been paid!

We have received an eternal inheritance (Hebrews 9:15) that cannot be taken away. Your inheritance is not temporary; it's eternal. You aren't disinherited, and you don't lose the benefits of being part of the family because of sin. To understand this, you have to see yourself as God sees you. In your born-again spirit, you are as clean and holy and pure as Jesus is.

Religion has you looking at your flesh. It has you searching the soulish realm of thoughts, attitudes, and feelings. But that is not what God is looking at. He is looking at your spirit, the part of you that's become a new creation.

Second Corinthians 5:17 says, *"Therefore if any man be in Christ, he is a new creature: old things are passed away; behold, all things are become new."*

In John 4:24 we read, *"God is a Spirit: and they that worship him must worship him in spirit and in truth."* An unbeliever doesn't need forgiveness of sin, what he/she needs is redemption by grace. When a person receives redemption through Jesus, it comes with forgiveness of sins as a bonus gift.

What part of you is new? It's not the flesh and it's not the soul; it's your born-again spirit. When you go to God in prayer and say "O God, I'm so ungodly and so unworthy, please forgive me, please answer my prayer," you are not in the spirit; you are in the flesh. Your spirit is righteous, holy, and pure. Sin does not affect your spirit.

Am I saying sin is okay? Absolutely not! When you sin, you give Satan an open door to the soul, your mind, and emotions, as well as opportunity to destroy your physical body. It's just stupid to open yourself up to the devil.

Some of you may still be thinking, Well, I know God died once for all men, but His sacrifice still must be applied whenever we sin. Let us allow God's Word to get in the way of this wrong theology again. Hebrews 10:10-12,14 reads *"By the which will we are sanctified through the offering of the body of Jesus Christ once for all. And every priest standeth daily ministering and offering oftentimes the same sacrifices, which can never take away sins: But this man, after he had offered one sacrifice for sins forever, sat down on the right hand of God; ...For by one offering he hath perfected forever them that are sanctified".*

These verses are not talking about your physical body or your soul; they are talking about your born-again spirit. Your spirit is identical to the Lord Jesus Christ. It is sinless! Your soul and your body can be defiled by sin, but your spirit never can; it's sealed forever.

An unbeliever doesn't need forgiveness of sin. What he or she needs is the redemption by Jesus Christ, and forgiveness of sin comes with the package of Redemption.

Maturity in the Christian life isn't about trying to grow your spirit up; it's trying to educate, or renew, your mind to what you already have in your spirit. Your spirit is already perfect! You already have the fruit of the Spirit—love, joy, peace, long-suffering, and the rest. Your spirit is always happy, always rejoicing, and always healthy.

God loves you even though you've messed up, even though you aren't perfect. He loves you not because of your performance but because of Jesus' sacrifice. If you can ever get a revelation of what I am teaching, it will change the way you see God forever.

Content #4: Adoption and a New Identity

The next important content in the package of redemption is adoption as sons and daughters of the living God and the idea that we have received a new identity, a new name, and new spirit. This is such a precious part of our redemption.

There are many Scriptures that talk gloriously of our adoption through Jesus Christ Death. Let's look at some of them.

Ephesians 1:5-6 (NIV) reads; *"He predestined us for adoption to sonship through Jesus Christ, in accordance with his pleasure and will-- to the praise of his glorious grace, which he has freely given us in the One he loves".*

Galatians 3:26 (NIV) reads, *"So in Christ Jesus you are all children of God through faith".*

Galatians 4:4-5 (NIV): *"But when the set time had fully come, God sent his Son, born of a woman, born under the law, to redeem those under the law, that we might receive adoption to sonship".*

Romans 8:14-17 (NIV) boldly declares: *"For those who are led by the Spirit of God are the children of God. The Spirit you received does not make you slaves, so that you live in fear again; rather, the Spirit you received brought about your adoption to sonship. And by him we cry, "Abba, Father." The Spirit himself testifies with our spirit that we are God's children. Now if we are children, then we are heirs – heirs of God and co-heirs with Christ, if indeed we share in his sufferings in order that we may also share in his glory.*

Romans 8:15 says, *"For ye have not received the spirit of bondage again to fear; but ye have received the Spirit of adoption, whereby we cry, 'Abba! Father!'".*

This verse contrasts two spirits: an impersonal "spirit of bondage" or "spirit of slavery" and the Holy Spirit, called here "the Spirit of adoption." Other translations render the phrase the Spirit of adoption as "God's Spirit when he adopted you as his own children" (NLT), "the Spirit makes you God's children" (GNT), or "a Spirit that shows you are adopted as his children" (CEB).

Two different spirits. Two different mindsets that we can have in our approach to God: we can approach Him as slaves in bondage, or we can approach Him as "adopted children." The Bible presents a high view of adoption and uses it to parallel the relationship God wants to have with us. The spirit of slavery views God as a slave owner with us as his trembling subjects. The spirit of adoption views God as a loving Father with us as His beloved sons and daughters in Christ.

A spirit of slavery is manifested in legalistic religion. Many cults and even some Christian denominations put such emphasis on rule-keeping that they instill fear and a sense of dread in their members. God is presented as a taskmaster who is never quite satisfied with anything we do.

The bar is always set a bit too high, so people find religious activities to keep themselves busy in the hope that God will accept them for their effort. Even those who have been born again through faith in Christ's sacrifice for their sin can cling to a spirit of slavery, never realizing the freedom that is theirs with the Spirit of adoption.

This spirit of slavery was rampant within the Jewish culture when Jesus came to earth. He soundly rebuked the religious leaders for instilling such legalism in people with whom God desired to have a loving relationship. (*See* Mark 7:7-9; Matthew 23:15-16).

Paul cautioned the early churches to be watchful for the return of that spirit of slavery. In Galatians 5:1 (NIV) he wrote, *"It is for freedom that Christ has set us free. Stand firm, then, and do not let yourselves be burdened again by a yoke of slavery."*

In astonishing contrast is the Spirit of adoption, the Holy Spirit of God who brings us into God's family. Jesus invited believers to address God as "our Father" (Matthew 6:8-9). God explained His desire to treat His people as sons and daughters. God has made this spiritual adoption possible through faith in His only begotten Son, Jesus Christ. (*See* John 1:12; 3:16-18; 14:6-7; & Romans 8:14). Based on our faith and confession of allegiance, God adopts us into His eternal family. See (Romans 10:9-10).

God, through the death of Jesus on the cross, had made us joint heirs together with Jesus Christ (Romans 8:17). We receive the Spirit of adoption when we accept, by faith, the grace that has been offered to us in Christ. It is the Spirit of adoption who teaches us to call out to God as our "Abba, Father."

There is a vast difference between the way sons serve their fathers and the way slaves serve their masters. Slaves may perform duties; sons perform acts of love. Slaves dutifully obey; sons gladly obey. Slaves are motivated by fear of punishment; sons are motivated by love of relationship. Slaves ask, "What is required?" Sons ask, "What else can I do for you?" The Spirit of adoption changes us from fearful slaves to joyful sons and daughters.

The Spirit of adoption allows us to "come boldly before the throne of grace" (Hebrews 4:16) as a beloved child runs to his father in times of trouble. Because of the Spirit of adoption, we can enjoy serving God without fear or obligation. Serving in our Father's kingdom becomes life's highest ambition (2 Corinthians 5:20).

You are a son and daughter of the one true God, the King and Creator of all that is living and dead, all that is seen and unseen, all the galaxies and planets. You are a royal VIP of Zion. Friend, stop acting like a slave and servant and start asserting your rights and dominion on Earth. The enemy has messed you up a lot. Now is the time for you to up your game and show him who is the real boss on this planet.

Content #5: The Blessing

Like every loving father, God has blessed all his children equally. Now, when I talk about the blessing, I'm not talking about your Range Rover or your 2004 Hyundai Sonata. It's funny how many of us and even some churches have relegated the blessing to only material things like cars, a house, or a good job.

In as much as I understand these things to be dear to many people's heart (myself included) these are not the main blessing. Why? Because you don't need God to buy a Range Rover. You don't need God to buy a nice house. What you need is a good job or to be a successful entrepreneur.

There are wealthy and rich unbelievers or people of other religions who don't believe in Jesus Christ but are very financially comfortable in life, even better than you and me. Therefore, cars, houses, and good jobs are not the blessings of God.

Whatever man can achieve by himself cannot be considered *the* blessing. So, when we think of blessing, we are looking at things that we can only access through the mercies and graciousness of God. When I talk of the blessings, I refer to things like

- Good Health
- Life itself
- Protection from the attacks of the enemy
- Children
- Healing and unmerited favor in the eyes of men.

But most importantly, there are spiritual blessings that we have received as part of the redemption package through Jesus Christ. What are spiritual blessings? Ephesians 1:3 says that we have been blessed with all spiritual blessings in Christ. What are these spiritual blessings, and what do they do for us? Contrary to some beliefs, they are not some mysterious power or cosmic connection reserved for a select few. They are the key benefits of a relationship with God through Jesus Christ.

The word blessing in Ephesians 1:3 is a translation of the Greek word *eulogy*, and it means "to speak well of." Since God is the one acting in this verse, we can say that God has spoken good things about us or pronounced good things for our benefit. The good things that God has decreed for us are probably beyond our ability to number, but we can outline a few by looking at the verses that follow the statement. (*See* Ephesians 1:4-13).

The first blessing listed is the election as saints. Ephesians 1:4 says that He has *"chosen us in him before the foundation of the world, that we should be holy and without blame before him in love."* God has chosen to make us holy and blameless and all because of His love, His good pleasure, and His grace (verses 5-6).

What a blessing, that "even when we were dead in sins" (Ephesians 2:5), God chose to extend His grace to us and offer us salvation. This is even more amazing when we realize that He made that decision before sin even entered the world. The second blessing listed is found in verse 5— our adoption as His children. Not only has God chosen us to be made holy, but He grants us full status as His children, with all the benefits thereof. John 1:12 says, *"As many as received him, to them gave he power to become the sons of God, even to them that believe on his name."* When we believe the gospel, we receive full access to the Father, able to call out to Him as His children.

The third spiritual blessing is in verse 6, where we are made *"accepted in the beloved."* The word "beloved" is related to grace and gives the idea of making us graceful or favorable through Christ, the beloved of God. When we put on Christ, the Father sees His loveliness when He looks at us. The blood of Christ has taken away the guilt of our sins, and we stand before the Father as perfectly accepted.

This leads us right into the fourth blessing, the redemption through His blood (Ephesians 1:7). Redemption speaks of buying one's freedom, paying a ransom. The price for our sins, the payment to buy us out of eternal condemnation, was fully paid by the blood of Christ. In Christ, we are no longer slaves to sin, but we become sons and daughter to God. Since we are bought and paid for by His blood, we have an obligation to glorify God in our body and spirit (1 Corinthians 6:20).

Verse 7 also describes the fifth blessing, the forgiveness of sins. It is closely related to redemption but looks at the other side of the coin. In paying the ransom for our sins, the debt of sin was canceled, and we were forgiven. We no longer have the burden of guilt for violating God's holy laws.

The sixth spiritual blessing listed is knowing the mystery of His will (Ephesians 1:8-10). God has given us wisdom and insight through His Word and has shown us His desire to bring all things together to glorify Christ. Since all of creation was made by Him and for His good pleasure (Revelation 4:11), the consummation of His plan is when everything and everyone is brought in line to glorify Him. By aligning ourselves with Him through faith, we become part of His perfect plan and purpose.

Verse 11 says that another blessing is the inheritance that is given to us through Christ. What is included in that inheritance? 1 Corinthians 2:9) reads, *"But as it is written, Eye hath not seen, nor ear heard, neither have entered into the heart of man, the things which God hath prepared for them that love him."* The riches of glory, the presence of

God, the eternal home – these don't even scratch the surface of all the blessings that belong to our inheritance.

Another blessing is found in Ephesians 1:13, which is the sealing of the Holy Spirit. When we become God's children, He places His mark of ownership on us, guaranteeing our eternal security. This is spoken of as the down-payment of our full redemption, to hold us until the day Christ brings us to Him. The list could go on and on speaking of the privileges that are ours in Christ. We are ambassadors bringing the message of reconciliation to a foreign land (2 Corinthians 5:20); and we are the bride of Christ. We have available to us the peace that passes understanding and the assurance that nothing can separate us from the love of God that is in Christ Jesus (Romans 8:39).

How do we access all these blessings? They are readily accessible to everyone who is in Christ Jesus. The way to be in Christ is by believing in the finished work of Jesus. When we believe that Christ died to take our punishment and now lives to give us new life, He grants us forgiveness of sins and all the blessings that accompany that salvation.

Friends, what amazing good news this is to us!! That we are not just saved, but that our salvation came with bundles of other benefits that we did not even deserve. All of us have received some good news in our life. Maybe somebody you care for told you they loved you. Maybe your test results came back negative or positive as the case may be. Maybe you received that promotion at work. Maybe you were approved for a home loan. Regardless of the situation, we all love to receive good news.

The news I just shared with you is greater than any good news you possibly could receive. This news has eternal ramifications, whereas most of the good news we receive is temporary. For example, a person may tell us they love us and another day that person tells us they no longer love us. Maybe we received negative test results but somewhere in the future our health takes a decline.

Maybe we received that promotion, but the company is struggling and has layoffs. Maybe we had the best intention of buying that new home, but we get hit with hardship and can no longer afford the mortgage payments. However, the Bible offers each one of us the Gospel which means "Good News." The reason the Bible is good news is because there is bad news. We all have been born into this world as sinners. A person who sins has missed the mark of holy perfection. You don't have to teach a child to lie. They lie of their own accord. You don't have to teach a child to be selfish, they come out screaming, "That is mine!" From the very beginning with Adam and Eve, humans have wanted to be independent of God. We all like to try to take control of our lives. We want to call the shots.

The apostle Paul had a great understanding of our Human Nature. He concluded: *"For I know that good itself does not dwell in me, that is, in my sinful nature. For I have the desire to do what is good, but I cannot carry it out. For I do not do the good I want to do, but the evil I do not want to do – this I keep on doing. Now if I do what I do not want to do, it is no longer I who do it, but it is sin living in me that does it. So I find this law at work: Although I want to do good, evil is right there with me."* (Romans 7:18-21, NIV).

You might be thinking, "I'm better than this person who has done this or that," or "I'm a good person." The problem is that we cannot measure how good we are or create a standard for what good is. (It would be an imperfect person creating such a standard) And how many elderly women would you have to walk across the street to be considered good?

The Bible says if we claim to be without sin, we deceive ourselves and the truth is not in us (1 John 1:8). Sin brings death. It may bring a physical death, but it definitely brings a spiritual death. The Bible tells us *"The wages of sin is death."* (Romans 6:23, NIV). But the 2nd part of that verse gives us a glimpse into God's heart: *"but the free gift of God is eternal life through Jesus Christ."* God, being our Creator, knows us better than anyone. And the great news is that God loves us! Romans 5:8, NIV reads, *"God demonstrates his own love for us in this: While we were still sinners, Christ died for us."*

God knew that we were sinners and decided to conquer that sin so we could be in right relationship with Him. *"God so loved the world that He gave His one and only Son, that whoever believes in him shall not perish but have eternal life."* (John 3:16, NIV). Jesus was the only human to live a sinless life. Jesus was the atoning sacrifice for our sins and the last sacrifice. His love didn't stop there because Jesus was resurrected three days later so that we may live with Him forever.

Life is not about us. Our life is a vapor. Life can be short and uncertain. But we can be certain of where we will go when we die. Life is about Jesus and our relationship with Him. Jesus is the only God to claim that he is truth, the way, and the life, and no one comes to the Father except through him (John 14:6). God offers us the free gift of eternal Life. You don't have to jump through all these hoops to get to Heaven.

You don't have to try to be perfect. Come as you are. Ephesians 2:8, NIV reads, *"For it is by grace you have been saved, through faith- and this is not from yourselves, it is the gift of God. "* You just need to believe and receive Jesus as your Lord and Savior.

CHAPTER 6

YOU ARE RIGHTEOUS AND HOLY

You are a baby and ignorant if you do not understand righteousness. You may have been in Church for thirty years but still a babe if you have not yet come to understand the word righteousness.

There is righteousness by faith in Christ and righteousness by works of the Law. Righteousness by works is more popular in many churches today than the righteousness by faith in Christ. No man ever obtained righteousness through the works of the law. If it was possible, then there would be no need for Jesus to come fulfill the law on our behalf.

The word "righteousness" has become a religious cliché that has lost its meaning to many people. Even Christians are confused about what righteousness is and how to receive it. This has left our society without a clear understanding of what it takes to have a relationship with

God. This is reflected in the moral collapse of our nations. It's imperative that we get back to the basics of righteousness.

"Righteousness" and its counterpart, "righteous," appear 540 times in 520 verses of the Bible. In contrast, "faith," "faithfulness," and "faithful" are only used 348 times in 328 verses. This means that there are 1.5 times as many Scriptures about righteousness as there are about faith. Righteousness is important.

A layman's definition of righteousness is simply "right standing with God." Righteousness is the condition of being in right relationship with the Lord. This can only happen through total faith and dependence upon Christ. There is no other way, and there is nothing we can add to our faith to obtain right relationship with the Lord (Romans 11:6).

One of the things that blinds people to a true understanding of righteousness is confusion about how we become right in the sight of God. It is commonly thought that our actions are the determining factor in God's judgment of our righteousness. That's not true. There is a relationship between our actions and our right standing with God, but right relationship with God produces actions, not the other way around. That is to say, we are not made righteous by what we do.

Righteousness is a gift that comes from the Lord to those who accept what Jesus has done for them by faith (Romans 5:17-18). The gift of salvation produces a changed heart that, in turn, changes our actions. Actions cannot change our hearts. It's the heart of man that God looks upon (1 Samuel 16:7). We must be righteous in our hearts to truly worship God.

The mistake of thinking that doing right makes us right is the same error the Pharisees made. Religion has always preached that if we clean up our actions, our hearts will become clean too. Jesus taught just the opposite (Matthew 23:25-26). It's through a changed heart that our actions change. The heart is the issue. Actions are only an indication of what is in our hearts. Actions are the fruit the heart produces.

Modern-day Christianity often puts the emphasis on actions instead of issues of the heart. This is reflected in Christians' excessive efforts to legislate change in people's actions instead of changing their hearts by preaching the Gospel. It's the Gospel that contains the power of God, not political action groups (Romans 1:16). Laws only affect actions. The Gospel changes hearts. Once hearts are changed, actions change.

Contrary to popular belief, Christianity does not promote receiving justice from the Lord. Praise God for that! The Lord has a much better plan. We get what we believe. I once worked in a photography studio for a living. Daily and especially at weekends, people would come into the studio to look at their proofs and say things like, "This picture doesn't do me justice." I never had the nerve to say this, but I often thought, "Lady, you don't need justice. You need mercy."

That's the way it is with God. We sometimes call for justice, but that's not what we need. As the Scriptures say, *"All we like sheep have gone astray; we have turned everyone to his own way; and the LORD hath laid on him the iniquity of us all."* (Isaiah 53:6). In Romans, the Scriptures say, *"There is none righteous, no, not one... For*

all have sinned, and come short of the glory of God."
(Romans 3:10, 23).

The wonderful plan of salvation is that those who put their faith in Jesus and what He did for us get what He deserves. On the other hand, those who do not put their total faith in Christ will ultimately get what they deserve. Believe me, that is not what they want. Religion has subtly instructed people to trust in their own goodness instead of God's. This will never work. For all have sinned and come short of the glory of God.

The Biblical story of the handwriting on the wall illustrates this point (Daniel 5:1-31). Belshazzar was the king of Babylon. His father, Nebuchadnezzar, had conquered the nation of Israel and brought all the wealth of the temple, along with most of the inhabitants of Jerusalem, back to Babylon. During an extravagant feast, with 1,000 of his lords in attendance, Belshazzar chose to toast his gods using the golden vessels from the temple in Jerusalem, which was an open defiance of the God of Israel.

The Lord moved swiftly and dramatically by creating an image of a man's hand, with fingers that wrote on the wall in front of Belshazzar and all his guests. Belshazzar called on all his magicians and wise men to decipher the writing, but none could. Then the queen reminded Belshazzar about Daniel, who had interpreted the dreams and visions of Nebuchadnezzar when no one else could. Daniel was summoned to interpret the writing.

The message from God revealed that Belshazzar had been weighed in the balances and was found wanting. Therefore, his kingdom would be divided and given to the Medes and Persians. This came to pass that very night.

Belshazzar was overthrown, and Darius, the Mede (Persian), took control.

If we were weighed in the balances against God's righteousness as Belshazzar was, we too would come up short. God's righteousness is always more in quantity and quality than ours will ever be. Our righteousness is as filthy rags compared to God's righteousness provided by Jesus. (Isaiah 64:6).

Someone might say, "That's not fair. No one can compete with God's righteousness." That's exactly right! However, God's righteousness is the standard by which everyone must be measured. So then, how can anyone be saved? The answer is that no one can be saved if they are trusting in their own righteousness. We all must have a righteousness that exceeds anything we could ever produce through our own effort. That's where Jesus enters.

Jesus is in right relationship with God as no one else can be. He is the Son of God. He is God manifested in the flesh (1 Timothy 3:16). He is holy and pure and without sin, yet He became sin for us, through no wrongdoing on His part (2 Corinthians 5:21).

He took our sin in His own body on the cross (1 Peter 2:24). Isaiah 53:4-5 declares *"Surely he hath borne our griefs,vand carried our sorrows: yet we did esteem him stricken, smitten of God, and afflicted. But he was wounded for our transgressions, he was bruised for our iniquities: the chastisement of our peace was upon him; and with his stripes we are healed".*

In return for Jesus taking our sin, those who put their faith in Him get His righteousness instead of their own. It's not our actions that make us acceptable to the Father. Our trust in Jesus imparts the righteousness of Jesus into our born-again spirits and makes us in right standing with God.

Those who don't understand this righteousness, which comes from God as a gift, become frustrated trying to establish their own righteousness through good works (Romans 10:3). It won't work. It's an all or nothing situation (Romans 11:6). We must trust completely in what Jesus did for us to obtain right relationship with God. Any trust in our own goodness will void the atonement Christ made for us (Galatians 5:4).

This is precisely the condition of millions of people in the body of Christ today. They receive salvation by putting total faith in Christ for the forgiveness of their sins, but then they return to believing that the Lord still relates to them based on their works, even after their salvation. That's not true.

Colossians 2:6 says, *"As ye have therefore received Christ Jesus the Lord, so walk ye in him."*. That means if you were saved by putting faith in God's grace alone, then you maintain that relationship in the same way. Some people sing "Just as I Am Without One Plea" when they are born again. They need to sing this song all the way through their Christian lives.

Failure to understand this truth is at the root of all guilt and condemnation. Satan's only inroad into our lives is sin. If we understand our right standing with God based on what Jesus did for us and not by our own actions, then Satan's power to condemn is gone. Those who live with a feeling of unworthiness are not trusting in God's righteousness but are looking to their own actions to obtain right standing with God. That will never work.

Most of the things we ask God to do are things He has already done for us in Christ on the cross. God never answers the prayers that ask Him to do things He has already done! This is a common reason why many believers seem not to have their prayers answered! Whatever we need for life and godliness has been done! The day you were born again, all that you will ever need in life was given to you! Your job is to receive! Receiving is faith!

First, the law was not given to non-Jews! The law was given to Jews, yet we non-Jews have become masters of borrowing the law which was not given to us and acting all religious about it. Ephesians 2:8 says, *"For by Grace Are You Saved."* The gospel is the gospel of the grace of God. The grace of Christ is the gospel. Under the covenant of grace, we don't get what we deserve! If we got what we deserved, we'd be in hell right now!

Faith only claims
what Grace has provided.

Faith takes, Grace makes! Faith takes what Grace made! Faith does not get God to make anything happen! God has made it happen. Faith only takes; it does not create! If grace has not created, then faith has nothing to take. When you fully understand the Grace of God, you will spend the rest of your life thanking Jesus Christ for His Goodness!

Guess where the message of Condemnation comes from most? The church!!! No wonder many do not have a genuine reason to attend church services! Most preaching in church focuses on sin rather than Christ. The reason why many struggle to see change is because they are trying to change their behavior instead of changing the concept of their identity! When we are born again, our nature changes. We have God's nature. When we were born in sin, we had the Satan nature, and we sinned just like he sinned. It didn't matter how much good we did; we were still sinners that sinned.

When you receive the life of God, you have His nature, a nature without sin. You are not a sinner anymore because He lives in you. There is no sin in Him, and if He be in you, there is no sin in you because He destroyed sin once and for all. You are pure just as he is pure. You have fellowship with Him because you are now the same.

Remember, sin is darkness and not light. If you are still in sin, you are still in darkness, and there is no fellowship between you and God. 1 John 3:1-9 tells us all about the clear difference of who you belong to. Verse 8 says that whoever sins belongs to the devil, and Jesus came to destroy the works of the devil, which was sin.

Righteousness is simply
right standing with God.

Think about this: doing right or wrong is not sin. Sin is a nature that you were born with. But when you confessed your sins, He forgave you, and you became a new creature. Old things have passed away. Now you are a new person; and a new person is not the same.

If you can still sin after being born again, then what did He take away? Don't you know that His blood is so powerful that you don't have to worry about sinning because it has been destroyed? He took it away. When God does something, He does it right. We just must believe that we are pure just like He is pure. He said He took sin away once and for all, but no one believes that because they are too busy looking at the wrong things they do, and they think that they are sinning again.

You do right and wrong whether you are born again or not, but the difference is you don't want to continue doing wrong. Why? Because you have God's nature. Before you had Christ, you were a sinner no matter what good or bad thing you did. Well, we must believe now that we are born again, that we are righteous, holy, and without fault and without sin in His eyes.

Is grace a license to sin?

The answer is No. No man needs a license to do evil. The fallen state of Man affords him that. Any man who is still a custodian of the Adamic Nature is a licensed sinner from birth. Sin is his nature. Grace is God's cure for sin. John the Baptist, the last prophet of the Old Testament, puts it like this: *"The next day John seeth Jesus coming unto him, and saith, Behold the Lamb of God, which taketh away the sin of the world."* (John 1:29) .

No man can defeat sin unless he beholds and receives this Lamb of God who is the embodiment of grace as the Bible says! *"And of his fulness have all we received, and grace for grace."* (John 1:16).

When a man receives Jesus, who is grace, Christ entering him, removes that sinful nature completely, and the nature of sonship takes over that man. He is no longer a sinner but a son of God! John 1:12 declares, *"But as many as received him, to them gave the power to become the sons of God, even to them that believe on his name.".*

Contrary to legalist claims, grace is the final cure for sin. When you receive grace – what Jesus the Lamb of God did in His death, burial, and resurrection – you automatically experience it and hence are adopted as God's child! *"For sin shall not have dominion over you: for ye are not under the law, but under grace."* (Romans 6:14). The Scriptures in Romans 5:20 also reads, *"Moreover, the law entered, that the offence might abound. But where sin abounded, grace did much more abound."*

Grace is the cure for sin.

Grace is not a license to sin. Grace is an Empowerment to reign over all the things we couldn't be free from under the Administration of Death (The Law)!!! An increase of sin cannot make Grace ineffective. The increase of the Revelation of Jesus (Grace) nullifies and makes Sin of no effect.

Grace is the cure for sin.

What makes men free is the knowledge of the truth, not struggling to behave right but the knowledge that Jesus Christ has revealed in the Scriptures. 1 Timothy 2:4 reads, *"Who will have all men to be saved, and to come unto the knowledge of the truth."* (). Why is the truth so important? It's important because Bible says so. *"And ye shall know the truth, and the truth shall make you free".*

So, what is the Truth?

The Truth is a Person. His name is Jesus Christ. He is Grace personified!!! Grace is a Person living His life through you. Jesus is the Truth that makes men free!!! This Freedom is evidenced by the workings of the law of the Spirit of Life in Christ Jesus whose power creates within you the desire to do His gracious will and brings about the accomplishment of that desire.

John 1:17 reads, *"For the law was given by Moses, but grace and truth came by Jesus Christ"*.

John 14:6 reads, *"Jesus saith unto him, I am the way, the truth, and the life: no man cometh unto the Father, but by me"*.

Philippians 2:12-13 reads, *"Wherefore, my beloved, as ye have always obeyed, not as in my presence only, but now much more in my absence, work out your own salvation with fear and trembling. For it is God which worketh in you both to will and to do of his good pleasure"*.

We only stumble when we shift our gaze from Jesus (The Author and Finisher of our faith). A believer that continues in the actions of sin is living in denial. He is suffering from identity crisis and double mindedness because he lacks a clear revelation of Jesus. Hence, he has mental agitation.

He has forgotten who he is and how he looks. *"For if any be a hearer of the word, and not a doer, he is like unto a man beholding his natural face in a glass: For he beholdeth himself, and goeth his way, and straightway forgetteth what manner of man he was."* (James 1:23-24).

When a believer is struggling with falling in sin, he/she is having an identity crisis. He needs the constant revelation of Jesus (GRACE) because that is what can unveil his true identity. 2 Corinthians 3:18 reads, *"But we all, with open face beholding as in a glass the glory of the Lord, are changed into the same image from glory to glory, even as by the Spirit of the Lord."*.

CHAPTER 7

THE SCRIPTURES THROUGH THE EYES OF JESUS

The Bible is a sacred book, containing in its contents one message: Jesus Christ. Hence, we say the Scriptures are Christo-centric or Christ centered. *"Search the scriptures; for in them ye think ye have eternal life: and they are they which testify of me."* (John 5:39).

Jesus is the explanation of all things in the Scriptures (Old Testament)!! Jesus Himself said so to us in Luke 24:25-27: *"Then [Jesus] said unto them, O fools, and slow of heart to believe all that the prophets have spoken: Ought not Christ to have suffered these things, and to enter into his glory? And beginning at Moses and all the prophets, he expounded unto them in all the scriptures the things concerning himself."*

Moses' and all the prophets' writings pointed to Jesus. The Scriptures will remain a mystery until you look at them through the eyes of Jesus' finished work on the cross. Stop looking at the Bible as Old and New Testament only but beyond that, as a revelation of the different dealings of God with Man through the ages, perfected in the appearance of Jesus.

Jesus is God's last word for the New Testament believer. Everything God said before and will ever say is Jesus Christ. The Old Testament is the agreement God had with Israel as a standard (in types and shadows) to point them to their helplessness and their need to believe in Jesus.

Jesus showed up, fulfilled the law (with all its requirements), and ended it for Man. Jesus is the end of the law. The Scriptures come to us two-fold: types/shadows and the reality. Colossians 2:17, (AMP) states, *"Such things are only a shadow of what is to come and they have only a symbolic value. But the substance (the reality of what is foreshadowed) belongs to Christ."*

Your walk as a Christian is only as effective as your understanding of the things that are yours in Christ. Remember, if your interpretation is wrong, your belief will be wrong, and so your practice will be wrong!

The Old Testament is Jesus concealed; the New Testament is Jesus revealed. You only understand the Old Testament through the revelation of Jesus. The Old Testament had types, shadows, prophecies, and promises. The New Testament is the fulfillment of all in Christ (Hebrews 10:1; Colossians 2:16-17).

*The Scriptures will remain a mystery
until you look at them through the
eyes of Jesus' finished work on the Cross.*

The Old Testament was given by angels, powered by the blood of bulls and goats (Galatians 3:18-20; Hebrews 2:2; Acts 7:35-36). The New Testament is powered by the blood of Jesus, given to us by Jesus (Hebrews 8:6). The Old Testament could never take away sin (Hebrews 10:1-4). The coming of Jesus took away sins. The Old Testament was a conditional testament (Deuteronomy 28:1 -3; Exodus 15:26).

In the New Testament, all conditions were met by Christ – for us, as our Lamb and High Priest, so we enjoy unconditional blessings in Him. The Old Testament justified no one (Romans 3:20; Galatians 2:15-16), but in the New Testament, Jesus justified us by faith in His blood (Romans 5:1-2). The New Testament is not in a book, but in the blood of Jesus. The New Testament has produced a new race, a new breed, the new Man, created in righteousness and true holiness.

The New Testament came by the grace of God, which teaches us how to live no more by the law of commandments but by the law of the Spirit of life in Christ Jesus, which has set us free from the (old) law of sin and death (Titus 2:11-12; Romans 8:2). Let's look at some Scriptures Galatians 2:21 reads: *"I do not frustrate the grace of God: for if righteousness come by the law, then Christ is dead in vain".*

Galatians 3:10-13 declares: *"For as many as are of the works of the law are under the curse: for it is written, Cursed is every one that continuth not in all things which are written in the book of the law to do them. But that no man is justified by the law in the sight of God, it is evident: for, The just shall live by faith. And the law is not of faith: but, The man that doeth them shall live in them. Christ hath redeemed us from the curse of the law, being made a curse for us: for it is written, Cursed is everyone that hangeth on a tree".*

Say out loud: "I put faith in Christ Jesus. I acknowledge and accept what He has done for me and in me, I am the new creation in Christ, I live in grace, I stand in grace, and His grace is enough for me! I am in Him justified; He is in me glorified! Amen!

1 John 2:2 clearly states that Jesus did what He did for the whole world! Not Christians alone! We who believe what Jesus has done call ourselves Christians or are called Christians, but that does not mean it was done for us only! It was done for the whole world.

John 3:16 proclaims that God so loves the world, you see! So, God had the world in mind at the cross! The world only needs to realize it and live in the reality of it. Outside the knowledge of what Jesus has done, there is the life of condemnation, sin consciousness, and guilt. Preaching the Gospel is designed to free people from that life and to introduce them to the liberty in the knowledge of Christ Jesus' finished works.

---

*Your walk as a Christian is only as effective
as your understanding of the things
that are yours in Christ.*

God has forgiven every man eternally in Christ. God Has redeemed every man in Christ. God Has justified every man in Christ. God has propitiated every man in Christ! Our job as people who have first believed is to tell others what God has done for them in Christ – that is called soul winning or evangelism.

It is not just a matter of a one-time conversation but taking time to teach and explain what God has done for them in Christ. The moment they understand and acknowledge this, they receive righteousness. Luke 24:25-27 has this to say; *"Then he said unto them, O fools, and slow of heart to believe all that the prophets have spoken: Ought not Christ to have suffered these things, and to enter into his glory? And beginning at Moses and all the prophets, he expounded unto them in all the scriptures the things concerning himself".*

Religion Is an Enemy of The Cross

Religion is working to gain what is freely given or trying to become what we already are. It is the best way to make Jesus unattractive and undesirable. Even though mankind is created to enjoy friendship with God, religion has caused our eyes to be blinded to the purpose and ultimate experience of life: to glorify God by enjoying Him forever.

The religious try to gain a heavenly status through their self-effort when all along, friendship with God would have made it clear to them that they already had a heavenly status. The problem with religion is that it always leaves you lacking. It always tells you there is more work to be done. It always demands something and doesn't lift a finger to help you out. It is the never-ending hamster wheel that keeps you running after the dangling carrot you will never catch.

God Is for Your Side

Even though we might have perceived our Father as our enemy due to a darkened understanding, He was never our enemy, and we were never His enemy. Adam's sin didn't alienate God from Adam; it alienated Adam from God. Paul says in Colossians 1:21 that we became enemies of God in our minds. God was never our enemy, but we sure thought He was.

God has always been our Friend/Father who has always been with us and close to us. Our inclusion in Christ's work on the cross has not only destroyed our sin nature but redeemed our image and likeness of God, thus restoring our friendship with God.

Sin did not change God's mind about us but our mind about God. God is not for you from the moment you come to faith, as if He was against you when you didn't believe. No, the truth is that God has always been our side.

He has always loved you. Likewise, He doesn't start loving you after you're saved as if He was angry before you woke up to His love... He's always loved you and will always love you simply because He is Love.

Even before you were lost through Adam, you were found in Christ. Thus, God has always been for you and has infinitely loved you, even before anything was created. In other words, everybody – Muslims, Hindus, Humanists, New-agers, Homosexuals – is already included in God's family (from God's perspective). However, not everybody is awakened to their inclusion in Christ. (By the way, I'm not talking universalism here but rather what the Bible reveals as being universal atonement).

*Sin did not change God's mind about us
but our mind about God.*

What if God is not against humanity? What if God loves everyone? What if Jesus cared about everyone regardless of what they believed about Him? What if God's love was unconditional? God cared about us when we didn't care about Him. God loves us all while we were still against having a relationship with Him. He demonstrated this through the death of Jesus on the Cross.

The Beginning of The New Testament

The differentiation of the Old Testament from the New Testament is not a function of time/arrangement of the texts but of an event. Knowledge of this will help you better understand certain supposed discrepancies in the Old scriptures.

I explained in previous chapters that Jesus is the central theme/message of the Scriptures. That's to say that all that was said or prophesied in the Scriptures was pointing to the death and resurrection of Jesus Christ. The events that separate the Old Testament from the New Testament are the death and resurrection of Jesus Christ. Therefore, the New Testament begins with the book of Acts. Why? Because at the beginning of the book of Acts, Jesus has died and resurrected, marking the beginning a new covenant and a new life.

Okay, now you are asking, "What about Mathew, Mark, Luke, and John?" Well, the four synoptic gospels are the transitional phase of the Scriptures because Jesus was still alive in the synoptic gospels. From our explanation above, they are therefore not part of the New Testament. The four gospels are documentations of Jesus ministry while on earth.

I would like you to understand that without the resurrection of Jesus from the dead, there would be no new convent and hence no New Testament either. In the synoptic gospels, Jewish laws and religious practices were still prevalent and consistently applied and observed even by Jesus himself.

The death and resurrection of Jesus marks the end of the Old Testament and the beginning of the New Testament.

Again what is righteousness? It is the right standing with God! What is right standing with God? It's a life lived in the acknowledgement of what God has done for him/her personally in Christ!

This righteousness (right standing with God) takes away every sense of guilt, condemnation, and inferiority! So, the result of receiving the gift of salvation is righteousness (right standing with God).

Have you ever asked the questions that get you in trouble at church? You know, the ones that pastors usually answer with a scowl on their faces saying, "Because the Bible says so, young man!" Those questions that come to the mind of every good Christian kid when he or she finally steps into a college class or sits in his/her room alone while all the friends go out and party. Questions like....

- If God is good, then why does everything seem so bad?

- If God is good, then why is He blamed for all the bad?

- If God is wonderful, then why do most Christians seem so miserable?

- How can I really be sure that I am "saved" by just believing?

- Is anyone actually "saved"?

- Did the cross work?

- If God is so loving, why did He love only the Israelites and allow the Egyptians to perish? Weren't the Egyptians created by God too?

- Was Christ's coming just a cosmic failure since most pastors say that most of the world is going to burn in hell?

- What is the point?!?!

I've asked all those questions, and I've gotten into some trouble for it among my believer friends and leaders. I've also come to a few conclusions that have dramatically changed the way I live life and love the people in my community. For most of you, the fact that you even picked up this book tells me that you probably fit into one of these categories namely:

- Normative Christian searching for a little clarity on how to be a better Christian and know God intimately.

- Failure Christian just trying to find something that might help keep you from losing your faith altogether.

- Zealous Christian looking for a deeper relationship with God.

- Dedicated Christian of Christian orthodoxy ready to underline and highlight all my errors.

- Former Christian who once believed in the God of the Bible but, due to life's circumstances and intellectual contradictions, has taken on more of an Agnostic position.

- Average folk looking for more purpose in life.

Humanity longs to worship something bigger than ourselves. We all long to see something or someone that will take us to our true origin. Kind of like a super-hero. Someone to save us, teach us how to become like the gods. Religion is all about mankind's desire to worship their gods and mankind's journey to become like their gods.

Every now and then, I find myself in conversations where genuine folks want to defend the validity of religion and present it as a helpful thing. They always say the word religion comes from the Greek phrase *thre skeia.* One of the meanings of the phrase is "the fear of gods." Really? The fear of the gods? Sounds fun to me.

For another meaning of the word, look at what Jesus said. He came to the woman at the well and told her, "I know that you Samaritans say worship services should happen at this mountain and that the Jews say that worship services should happen at a different mountain, But let me tell you a little secret Jesus replied, the whole earth is full of glory, and true worship is done by those who recognize that heaven is not only here or now, but God is here and now. You're in Him and He's in you" (John 4:5-26; Luke 17:21)

How in the world are we supposed to package a religion like that? God living inside of us. Rushing rivers of God-life right smack-dab in the middle of our bellies. This can't be controlled. That's the point of religious control. The law is the only tool through which people are easily controlled and make themselves lords over others in the body of Christ.

Are the practices of external ceremonies and worship right? It seems like the inside of the heart is more important than the external motion of worship that someone may or may not perform. Even so, what we do does matter, in a sense. It matters because we were made to love, and love always has an expression.

That is the entire point of the little Bible verse about true religion. I can almost imagine James speaking tongue-in-cheek, "Ladies and gents, I know that we come from a deeply religious culture. Our entire history is full of external ceremonies and rituals that we love so dearly."

Through the law, God met Man on our terms. We didn't want relationship; we wanted rules. God's original intention has always been a love relationship, not forced obedience. When God created Adam and Eve, He didn't set up a bunch of rules for them to follow. He said, "Be fruitful and multiply. And don't eat from the tree of the knowledge of good and evil. (Now that's a good deal!) Guys, go enjoy one another and enjoy the garden I gave you! Oh, and don't sit around wondering about right and wrong. That's actually none of your concern."

There are many different definitions of religion, but I'll go with this one: working to gain what is freely given or trying to become what we already are. The Jews had this same problem. For thousands of years they studied the law and sought to keep it perfectly, and many of them thought they did.

There was absolutely nothing wrong with the law. The law was good. But the law was never God's original intention for mankind. The law was not introduced to save Man but rather to show Man his weakness and need for a savior.

Before the law, there was no sin as a verb (i.e. there was no sin as a result of human deeds, actions or behavior). Before the law of Moses, sin was not a function of lies, stealing, or any other human behavior. From Adam to Abraham, Isaac, Jacob, and Joseph, there was no sin as a verb. Sin in the times of these patriarchs was the cause of the fall. Let me simplify this a bit.

In the times of these people, there was no such thing as lying, stealing, or cheating. Why? Because there was no law of Moses then to impute such fault. So, they had no knowledge of sin as an action.

Chopping Down That Ole' Tree

The Tree of the Knowledge of Good and Evil is exactly that, trying to figure out what is good and what is evil. God doesn't want us messing around with that kind of thinking. He has something so much more enjoyable for us! Jesus called it life and life abundantly. Religion has created an industry based on figuring out what's right and wrong. We were never supposed to spend our time thinking about rights and wrongs. We were made right with God when we were created. God's one command was that we would remember who we really are and where we come from.

When we dug into that malnourishing meal from the ole' tree of religion, we believed the lie of the enemy. What was that lie? That we must become like God, as though somewhere along the way we were no longer like Him.... But that was the lie: that God didn't really make us in His image and likeness. *"Let us make man in our image and in our likeness"* (Genesis 2).

The enemy came to Eve and accused God of withholding something from mankind and making us less than perfect. Then of course, he convinced her that the only way to become like God was to have their eyes opened to light and darkness, good and evil, right and wrong. Once Adam and Eve ate of that tree, they realized that they were basically in a nudist colony. This wasn't "wrong" before. But when sin entered the picture, their lack of clothing became nakedness. That's why God asked them the question, "Who told you that you were naked?"

The glory that clothed them before the fall was still there, but their eyes had been blinded to the truth. God saw perfection; they saw nakedness. God saw beauty; they saw blemishes. Relax, I'm not trying to promote nudist colonies. What I am saying is that God has seen us as a perfect reflection of His image from the very beginning. There was nothing we could do to add to that and nothing we had to do to gain acceptance from him. We were covered by His glory until we were told that we were naked and incomplete.

Adam and Eve chose to eat the fruit of that tree and had their eyes opened to a burden that they were never meant to carry. God's original intent for mankind was that we live life and live it abundantly, be good and see good all around us. He never wanted us to have to live trying to figure out right and wrong, good and evil. Don't taste, don't touch, etc. (*See* Colossians 2). These commands come from the religion. We were never made for that tree.

We were made for the tree of life. That was the only tree we were made to eat from. It's time to chop down that ole' tree of right and wrong, good and evil. It's time to eat from the tree of life: Jesus Himself. This Tree is full of life and light. In that Tree, there is no death and no darkness. Eating from the Tree of Life only produces more life and more love. This is what true living is about.

Jesus Frustrates the Religionist

Jesus is such a funny dude. Seriously, as soon as you think you have Him figured out, He does something or says something that is completely opposite of what you had concluded about Him. This is what happened to the Pharisees when He showed up.

Can you imagine? The Pharisees had spent their lives studying the character of God and the attributes of the coming Messiah. They knew when he was coming, and they knew what he would do. They created systems and structure to explain and contain him.

But when Jesus came on the scene, these guys found out that He didn't fit in with their systems and structures at all. In fact, He broke their rules and ended up spending most of his time with the screw-ups and the folks that the systems had condemned as unclean. Unlike the religionist, Jesus didn't come to nit-pick at their lifestyles. Instead, He came to remind them that they were heavenly offspring, loved by a Dad who was willing to die for them.

The religionists had studied the law so intently that they even came up with new law that helped explain what God must have really meant when He gave the law. They created laws on top of laws and commands within commands.

The law said, "Rest on the Sabbath" The religionist said, "Don't do anything on the Sabbath". The law said, "Be generous and give a tithe." The religionist said, "Even if your family is struggling and needs that money to survive, you should still give us your money and let your family starve".

Jesus came and rebuked the religious folk, reminding them that the whole point of life was love. Man wasn't made for man. But the religious mind always takes what was meant to serve us and turns it in to a god – imagining that by serving this law, they are somehow pleasing God.

Jesus came on the scene and told the poor widow that she was amazing for giving all that she had when the Pharisees sneered at her for not giving enough. The way a religious person judges other, is a good clue about the way he judges himself. The work is never finished, and what is given is never enough.

Jesus disciples did some "harvesting" on the Sabbath to grab a bite to eat, and Jesus didn't care at all. The Pharisees rebuked Jesus for not rebuking His boys over the matter. Jesus told them that even in the old covenant David broke the law and it was no big deal (*See* Matthew 12:1-8 & 1 Samuel 21:6).

Again, the Pharisees showed up to get Jesus in trouble when He fixed a dude's hand on the Sabbath. Jesus totally healed the bro. But wait, it was on the Sabbath, and I'm sure that healing took some kind of boldness. I can only imagine Jesus looking at those Pharisees sarcastically saying, "Guys, if you were sitting at home on the Sabbath in your favorite Chesterfield and you got a text from your friend saying that someone stole your car, then I guarantee that you'd be out of that chair faster than you can say, 'Save us Lord.' "If you'd take care of your property like that, then how much more should I take care of My human race every single day of the week! Love isn't work for Me; it's as easy as breathing. And My Dad and I never stop loving humans...... You shouldn't either."

Jesus Doesn't Mind You Making Mistakes

Jesus didn't care to follow the religious rules, and He wasn't impressed with those who claimed to keep all of them. In fact, when people boasted in their flawless rule keeping, Jesus made up new rules for them. "Oh, you're good at rules? Cool I'm the guy who made them, so I can make a few more for you since you enjoy them so much." Check out what Jesus said to this rich guy who asked him how to get eternal life:

Matthew 19:17b-22 (The Living Bible) reads, *"'You can get to heaven if you keep the commandments.' 'Which ones?' the man asked. And Jesus replied, 'Don't kill, don't commit adultery, don't steal, don't lie, honor your father and mother, and love your neighbor as yourself!' 'I've always obeyed every one of them,' the youth replied. 'What else must I do?' Jesus told him, 'If you want to be perfect, go and sell everything you have and give the money to the poor, and you will have treasure in heaven; and come, follow me.' But when the man heard this, he went away sadly for he was very rich."*

Did you catch that? Jesus just made up a brand-new commandment for the guy. Can you imagine looking at God and saying, "Yep I did all that stuff that you said. What else have you got for me, Lord?" So, Jesus speaks with the man on his own terms, "Well, little buddy, since you've been a good boy, I will give you one more challenge. Sell all your stuff; give away all your money; and come follow me. Then you'll be saved, got it?" Then the man walked away discouraged because he finally heard a command that he couldn't keep.

This religionist couldn't handle the command. Thankfully, the story doesn't end there. If we take another look through the lens of grace and love, we might find that it ends on a positive note. The disciples, being sharp as they were, spoke up and said "Jesus! Wow, that was intense. Man, you really told that guy. He just couldn't hack it, I guess he couldn't handle the heat. Nope, not like us. We left everything to follow you. Yep everything. So...we're good right?"

Ummmm......

Jesus answered, "Guys it is really tough for the rich man to be saved. In fact, it's easier to park a Mack-truck in a compact car parking space than for man to be saved." [GASP!] "Then who can be saved. Jesus?!?!?!?" cried the disciples. (That's the whole point, right? Who can be saved?) Finally, Jesus could get to the punch line. "Well, if it's up to you guys and your rule-keeping, religious efforts and your good-boy to-do list.... Umm, pretty much, no one. In fact, I want you to fail. I want you to fail at religion. But, if it's up to me, then absolutely nothing is impossible, and the doors are open to everyone."

The point of this story was not that we would all feel bad for the rich man and think, "Wow, Christianity is only for spiritually tough guys who will be broke enough for Jesus." It may sound spiritual, but it's not the gospel. The guy who had the most hope of being saved in this story is the guy who walked away realizing that he couldn't save himself.

Did you get that? The rich dude finally had come to the end of himself. Jesus couldn't have set him up for the gospel any better. I can only imagine the guy thinking "Gosh, I have done everything perfect my whole life, I just dropped the ball. I'm not perfect anymore. I guess I can't be saved. I quit!" And of course, Jesus probably thought, "Finally, he failed. Now he can realize that he never needed to try in the first place. I am his origin. I am his perfection, and I am his salvation."

CHAPTER 8

KNOWING GOD AND HIS WORD ABOUT YOU

The major problem for a believer or unbeliever is not sin or Satan, neither is it Hell fire. The greatest problem or enemy of Man is his ignorance of the finished works of Jesus Christ or his or her misinformation about Jesus. Throughout history, there have been misconceptions and misunderstandings about the personality of God. We will look at this more in detail as we progress ahead.

Ignorance is the devil's greatest tool/weapon against any man. Therefore, the devil's greatest asset in a man's life is his mindset. The devil has no power over any human being. He needs your permission to influence your thoughts or actions. Any area of your life that the enemy seems to have control over is the area where you lack knowledge of the Truth.

In the church today, many are more knowledgeable about Satan and his works than they are about Jesus and His works in their lives. This is the origin of all spiritual turmoil in a man's life. I would like you to understand that Satan is a powerless deity. The only power he possesses is the power you give to him ignorantly.

If you think him to be powerful, he will surely manifest himself powerfully in your life. If you think him to be the powerless, defeated fool (not to mention liar) he is, that is surely what he will always be in your life. You have less of Satan and his works by knowing more of Jesus. That is to say, the more of Jesus you know, the less Satan influences your life. The devil plays a mind game with us, and that is why the Scriptures admonish us in Romans 12:2 saying, *"And be not conformed to this world: but be ye transformed by the renewing of the mind."*.

The more of Jesus you know
The less of the enemy influences your life.

Not every message that is sensible is truth. We are not products of feelings but of resurrection. Living by your feelings is a sign that you are not growing in spiritual things. You must grow out of feelings into faith. When you are controlled by feelings, it is an indication that you are a sense-ruled, sense-dominated Christian.

You are the type referred to as "carnal." A Christian is described as carnal when he/she is governed by his senses (1 Corinthians 3:1). His senses dictate his actions, as his mind is not regulated by the Word of God. Anything Satan throws at him becomes effective, and he cannot live in victory (1 Corinthians 5:7). But when you grow in grace, you walk in knowledge and not feelings.

An unbeliever is not carnal. The term "carnality" is associated with believers, not unbelievers. An unbeliever is not carnal because he/she is yet to accept Jesus Christ as his/her Lord and Savior. 1 Timothy 2:3-4 reads, *"For this is good and acceptable in the sight of God our Savior; Who will have all men to be saved, and come unto the knowledge of the truth."*

Receiving the knowledge of God is the indication that you are growing in spiritual things. Satan does his best to keep you from knowledge of God in order to keep you in bondage, but Jesus says, *"And ye shall know the truth, and the truth shall make you free."* (John 8:32).

Ignorance of the Word of God and what Jesus had done for you through the Cross is the enemy's greatest tool against your life.

There was a time in my life when I was very ignorant of the Scriptures and did not even understood what the Cross meant. I read my Bible daily, did my quiet time, attended services in church. I was a committed church goer. I held several leadership positions in my local churches back then, but I lacked an in-depth understanding of the significance of the finished works of Jesus Christ in my life.

I mean, I knew He died for me, but I just did not understand the significance of His death, burial, and resurrection in my life. And this was due to the doctrinal teachings I was exposed to. Doctrines that, to my knowledge now, are unscriptural and wrong.

Doctrines like a woman should not wear trousers or expose her hair while in church, Doctrines like God is angry at you if you are in sin, or that if I don't tithe, I'm cursed. Doctrines like I must live a sinless life in other to gain salvation and holiness. Doctrines like you must dress in a certain way or else you are a sinner and a prostitute. And the females were more affected by this doctrine. Young girls were made to dress like old women in the name of being Holy.

Doctrines like television, cell phones, and social media are instruments of the Devil. Doctrines that said if you drink alcohol or smoke cigarettes, you are going straight to Hell Fire. My deceased Daddy was a smoker and a heavy one at that, but he was a believer also. When he died, one of the reasons for my prolonged sadness and pains from his death was the idea that he was burning in Hell fire since he was a smoker and had frequently gotten drunk. Lol!! Oh, poor me.

How ignorant I was! Thank God for renewed knowledge! I'm confident now that my beloved father is in heaven singing praises and worshipping with the angels because he died as a believer that Jesus Christ is his Lord and Savior, and that is the only requirement to gain eternal life, not his lifestyle or bad behaviors.

And you know the funny part of this whole saga was that you dare not rebel or challenge this doctrinal stands, because if you do, you are tagged a backslider, a sinner, a carnal man/woman. They will even call you a candidate for Hell fire. Some might excommunicate you from the church or relegate you to the back seat in the auditorium, so the entire church can see how bad you are.

These were the types of Doctrinal teachings I grew up with in the body of Christ in my West African country of birth. Every day, I was always worried about the security or assurance of my salvation, constantly feeling guilty for all the wrongs and bad things I did each day, and the truth is, it was often.

The moment I sinned; I began to ask God for forgiveness. I was always asking for forgiveness, and it never stopped because I kept doing the same thing I asked to be forgiven of. I kept going back to the same mess. I was told that God was angry at me for all the sins I committed. I was told by my pastors that my sinful life was the reason I was failing academically, in business, and in my personal life. Deep down in my heart I knew I was never going to make heaven without knowing that my God so loved me even in my messed-up state of life.

Thank God I have been saved from these lies. I now know the truth. What is that truth? The truth is that my salvation is secured. The truth is that God is not angry at me, neither is He looking for ways to harm me. He is not the one behind all my misfortunes in life.

The truth is that God loves me more than I love myself. The truth is that Jesus Christ, through His death and resurrection, has forgiven all my sins past, present, and future. The truth is that there is nothing I can do to earn redemption, but it was given to me as a gift.

The truth is that I am loved by God, and my mistakes and weakness in life are not held against me in judgment. The truth makes men free! When the truth makes you free, you are a free man. Nothing changes that. Paul would later write to his protégé Timothy, saying, *"Ever learning, and never able to come to the knowledge of the truth."* (2 Timothy 3:7).

Jesus is the truth. The more we know Jesus, the more we are exposed to the truth. Learning about Christ is required of a believer in order to fully function in the reality of the finished work of the Cross.

Satan hides in the darkness of the believer's ignorance to perpetuate evil. The darker it is with a believer, the stronger his dominion over that life. To overcome the domination of the senses, you must grow in the knowledge of God. You do not know God by feeling or sight, you know God by His word. You are not what you feel but what you know and hence believe.

It is for the purpose of knowing God that God inspired the writing of the Scriptures. Timothy 3:16-17 reads, *"All scripture is given by inspiration of God, and is profitable for doctrine, for reproof, for correction, for instruction in righteousness: that the man of God may be perfect, thoroughly furnished unto all good work."*

To be furnished is to be equipped. The Word of God equips us for every good work. It is the source of spiritual power required to affect good works. What are good works? They are works that reverse the works of Satan. Peter said, *"How God anointed Jesus of Nazareth with the Holy Ghost and with power: Who went about doing good and healing all that were oppressed of the devil; for God was with him."* (Acts 10:38).

Good works are works of dominion; they are the acts of God through us. God wants us to be mature to be able to do good works. Without the knowledge of God, we will not be effective in fulfilling the will of God on the earth. Revelation 12:10-11 reads, *"And I heard a loud voice saying in heaven, Now is come salvation, and strength, and the kingdom of our God, and the power of his Christ: for the accuser of our brethren is cast down, which accused them before our God day and night. And they overcame him by the blood of the Lamb, and by the word of their testimony; and they loved not their lives unto death".*

The Bible identified three things in the above bible passage that I want us to take note of.

The accuser of our brethren that accused them day and night before God

The accused that were accused before God day and night

They (the accused) overcame him (the accuser) by the blood of the Lamb and by their testimony

There is an accuser on the loose. His weapon is accusation, and he must be overcome. You cannot overlook the accuser. You must confront him and overcome him. In addition to overcoming the accuser, we need to overcome the accusation with which the accuser accuses us. A believer that does not know this will live a defeated life. He will struggle in his faith life because he lacks the assurance of his salvation.

There won't be victory until we know what God did for us in relation to the accusation of the accuser. They overcame him [the accuser] by the Blood of the Lamb and by the words of their testimony; and they loved not their lives unto death. They overcame the fear of death, stood their ground on the provision of the blood of Christ, and kept to the word delivered unto them.

The phrase "the word of their testimony" in that passage of the Bible does not refer to the testimonies about material gains people speak about in church services. Some of those testimonies are either exaggerated or outright lies. Nobody overcomes by them. The testimony that overcomes the devil is the testimony of the evidence of the sufferings of Christ and His resurrection from the dead.

When you do not know the provision of the sacrifice of Jesus, when you do not know what God says about what Satan is accusing you of, you remain vulnerable to Satan. You do not overcome the accuser by prayers and fasting; you overcome him by the knowledge of God.

No More Condemnation

The word "accuser" or "accusation" conveys a petition against someone by an adversary. Of course, it is obvious that God cannot be the accuser. We plead our case to God. Who would God petition if He is the accuser? God is the highest authority there is. He petitions nobody about anybody or anything. Romans 8:1 reads, *"There is therefore now no condemnation to them which are in Christ Jesus, who walk not after the flesh, but after the Spirit*

He is the eternal end of all things. God is not against us. He could not be against us and still make the provision for our salvation, He did that when we were still in sin. Romans 5:8 reads, *"But God commendeth his love toward us, in that, while we were yet sinners, Christ died for us."*

He died while we were dead in sin. There was no life in us when He went to the cross for us (it is a blessing). But now that we are reconciled to God through the blood of Christ, it is certain that we are secured from the wrath to come.

You overcome the enemy not by prayer and fasting but by a renewed knowledge of the Word of God about you.

If God did not condemn us when we were dead in sins, when we were enemies, but reconciled us by the death of Christ, how could He turn around to condemn us now? Christ's life is our salvation, which is our protection from the accuser and his accusation. Romans 5:10-11 reads, *"For if, when we were enemies, we reconciled to God by the death of His Son, much more, being reconciled, we shall be saved by his life. And not only so, but we also joy in God through our Lord Jesus Christ, by whom we have now received the atonement".*

We rejoice in God through our Lord Jesus Christ by whom we have now received the atonement. "Atonement" is an Old Testament concept that means bringing two warring parties together in an agreement for peace. It is written as "at-one-ment." It is a form of agreement or a covenant of peace which was usually sworn over blood. The New Testament calls it "reconciliation" with God through the blood of Christ.

This is a stronger concept than atonement. God took an oath over the blood of Christ to be at peace with every one that comes to Him through Christ Jesus. Now that we have been reconciled to Him through Christ, we shall be saved from the wrath and come to His life. There is nothing the believer can ever do that God will be so angry with you that He will reverse what He did for you in Christ Jesus. He did what He did to save you when you were in the worst state that a man could ever be: the fallen state.

There is nothing Satan can do about this. There is no level he can push you to that you will be irredeemable. Jesus already paid the price. The worst place anybody can be is Hell, and Jesus went there for us. He has redeemed us from it, and there is now therefore NO CONDEMNATION for those who are in Christ Jesus. The opposition does not have wherewithal to judge us.

God is not against you – not Today,
Tomorrow, nor Forever.

The word "condemnation" is used in legal terms to indicate a verdict. It is the same as damnation. Condemnation is the actual judgment. When the court of law condemns a man, it means he is judged guilty and sentenced to serve the required punishment as written in the law.

So, when the Bible says there is therefore no condemnation for those who are in Christ Jesus, it means there is no judgment for those who are in Christ Jesus. They have been declared by the blood of Christ as "not guilty," so no sentence and no punishment!

There is nothing like "God will get you." God is not looking for you because you are not lost. You are in Christ. God already knows where you are. He is not against you and He is certainly not looking for ways to get you.

When people do not know the Word of God, they are cut off from the ways of God. Until you understand the Word of God concerning salvation, you cannot think like Him about salvation. Without a full grasp of God's love, you will live your life in the shadows, and that life will have no meaning.

Freed by Righteousness

Romans 5:16-18 reads, *"And not as it was by one that sinned, so is the gift: for judgment was by one to condemnation, but the free gift is of many offences unto justification. For if by one man's offence death reigned by one; much more they which receive abundance of grace and of the gift of righteousness shall reign in life by one, Jesus Christ. Therefore, as by the offence of one judgment came upon all men to condemnation; even so by the righteousness of one the free gift came upon all men unto justification of life."*

One man sinned, and it brought the condemnation of death upon all Man. Death reigned through Adam. On the same premise, Jesus introduced righteousness into the human spirit, that many shall have the justification of life through Him. Adam sinned, and it condemned all men to death. Jesus obeyed, and it brought justification of life upon all men. Through righteousness, justification was imputed upon all men that believed.

None of this was a result of a direct action by you or anybody. It was Adam's action, his disobedience, that brought sin to Man and death by sin, and that made us sinners. In the same way, it was Jesus's action, His obedience, that brought righteousness upon Man.

It is not what we did in either of these cases. We were made sinners by the disobedience of Adam, and we were made righteous by the obedience of Christ. Once you are in Christ, righteousness frees you from sin. Like I said earlier, righteousness is the state of being right. It is a state where you are treated as someone who has not done any wrong. In that state, God treats you as though you have never sinned. When the Bible says you are righteous, it is not saying your works are perfect or that there are no flaws in your life, but that God is treating you as someone who has not done wrong.

If that is how God treats and relates with you, then you must stop acting like a criminal. You will only be a pretender acting that way, and that is living a false life. If you have received Christ as Lord, then live your real life, which is a "not guilty" life.

Stop walking and acting like a thief that is yet to be caught. Stand in the boldness of righteousness, and act as though sin never happened. Yes act.

Righteousness is a gift; you did not earn it. It was not given to you because you stopped doing something wrong. It was given because you received the gospel. The gospel of Jesus Christ. The gospel is the power of God unto salvation. When you receive the gospel, you receive power that saves you and keeps you safe.

The gospel brings the gift of "no condemnation" into your life. That is what makes the gospel good news. The state of no wrong, so no sentence. That is good news! That is what makes Christianity the greatest and best life to ever live.

Legally, doctrinally, and intellectually, there is no wrong established against you. Therefore, there is no condemnation and thus, no sentence. There is no judgment for a righteous man because he's been justified by Christ. Justification is the legal word for righteousness, and it is a gift.

Some teachings suggest that there are certain steps to take in order to become righteous. They make altars for believers to come and cry on the altar and afflict their souls. They teach foundation classes and baptismal classes for people to attain justification, etc. While there is nothing wrong in teaching foundation classes to help young believers develop in Christ or crying before God, you do not have to take any steps to attain righteousness because it is a gift.

There are no steps to take to receive a gift! It is a gift that comes when you believe the gospel and receive Christ into your life as Lord and Savior. The gift of life does not require conditions to be kept, you just receive it by faith. You do not have to feel like it. You do not have to deserve it, but just take it by faith. The Bible says, *"For by grace are ye saved through faith; and that not of yourselves: it is the gift of God: Not of works, lest any man should boast."* (Ephesians 2:8-9).

Salvation is the gift of God; it is the grace of God. There is no boasting because none of us deserved it. We did not work for it. Jesus did. Isaiah says your righteousness is like filthy rags. "Filthy rags" refer to menstrual cloths, a defilement under the Law of Moses.

Depending on moral uprightness is a sin. It is filthy. When God looks at your works, they are filthy. They stink. That was why God chose to redeem us by Himself and clothed us in His righteousness, so that we stink no more.

All "self-made" preaching is a defilement; we must depend on the work of grace and not all these man-made doctrines of wearing this or not wearing that. If dress codes or morality could save people, Jesus would not have needed to go to the cross.

Why would Jesus pass through such a painful and humiliating death if dress codes could give eternal life? The people teaching such things are grossly ignorant of God's Word. Paul says, *"And be found in Him, not having mine own righteousness, which is of the law, but that which is through the faith of Christ, the righteousness which is of God by faith."* (Philippians 3:9).

Another thing we need to understand is that righteousness is not a reward. It is not a payment for good works or a crown for winning in a competition or something similar. It is God's gift. You do not pray for it, and you do not "faith" for it. No amount of prayer and fasting can make you righteous or holy.

No style of dress makes anybody righteous. It is the grace of God, so the Bible calls it the gift of righteousness. Righteousness was given to secure us from judgment. The Word of God says, *"In righteousness shalt thou be established: thou shalt be far from oppression; for thou shalt not fear: and from terror; for it shall not come near thee."* (Isaiah 54:14).

*Righteousness is not a reward or payment
for good deeds. It's a Gift.*

Righteousness secures us from oppression and protects us from fear. You will not be bold to confront the enemy if you are not established in righteousness. Whatever God did for us, it is His righteousness speaking. The Bible says the righteousness of God speaks (Romans 10:6-8). Redemption in the blood of Christ is the voice of righteousness. God would have to be unrighteous to undo it because of Christ's righteousness, and we have redemption through His blood just as Colossians informed us ,in" Colossians 1:14: *"In whom we have redemption through His blood, even the forgiveness of sins*

Forgiveness of sin is not what God did before He saved us. It is not an answer to our prayer. Forgiveness of sins is factored into redemption. God provided that for us as part of our security after we received salvation. You were not forgiven because you confessed your sins. Confession of sins does not save anybody.

*Forgiveness of sin is not an answer to prayer
but a part of Redemption.*

Men confessed their sins in Old Testament, but none were saved. Confession of sins is not a requirement for salvation. The Bible says, *"That if thou shalt confess with your mouth the Lord Jesus, and shalt believe in thine heart that God hath raised him from death, thou shall be saved."* (Romans 10:9).

Through the redemption that we have in Christ Jesus, we have been secured from condemnation. The believer is free from judgment. He has the life of God in him. Eternal life cannot be judged. There is therefore now no condemnation to those who are in Christ Jesus. It does not cost fasting and prayers to be in Christ Jesus; it costs absolutely nothing to be in Christ Jesus. You only need to believe and confess Christ's Lordship over your life, and you shall pass from death to life.

This is the simple truth of the Bible, which to many legalistic people is a mystery. How can a person believe, and he is saved just like that? How can you do nothing and yet God still loves and blesses you? These are some of the questions religious folks just don't buy into.

CHAPTER 9

OVERCOMING SIN CONSCIOUNESS

Many believers are defeated in the area of sin consciousness. E.W Kenyon said, "The greatest problem of the church is not sin, but sin consciousness." The Scriptures in 1 John 3:19-20 reads, *"And hereby we know that we are of the truth and shall assure our hearts before him. For if our heart condemns us, God is greater than our heart, and knoweth all things."*

Why will your heart condemn you when the Scripture says no condemnation? As we discussed in the previous chapters, there is no need for further sacrifices to be made to atone for any sin. Our acts of obedience to God are not sacrifices that pay for sin – whereas in the Old Testament, the sacrifice of a valuable animal was a necessary and required faith step for the people's sins to be covered. Such sacrifices are no longer required, as Christ fully provided through His own body and blood all the sacrifices needed for atonement.

---

*"The greatest problem of the Church is not sin,
but sin consciousness". ~E. W Kenyon*

God no longer remembers sins which are under the blood of Christ, and furthermore, God certainly doesn't want us to be conscious of guilt for those things which Christ has paid for. Today, the worshipers the Father seeks should have no consciousness of sin. Why? Because the Father is seeking those who worship in spirit and in truth (See John 4:23-24).

The Father is not seeking unfaithful hypocrites, idolaters, or lovers of uncleanness to give Him lip service. Those He calls to stop deceiving themselves and repent. Worshipers should come with faith and total acknowledgment of their inability to please God by the deeds of their works or morality.

God wants worshipers with humility and with dependence on the Spirit of God. These people are pleasing to God because they are in Christ and have been sanctified. These are the people who believe that God is a rewarder of those who diligently seek Him (Hebrews 11:6). They have that faith without which it is impossible to please God, as the Scriptures have admonished us.

As for those who worship with their lips while their hearts are full of greed, lust, and impurity, who say, "I love you, Lord" when really they don't – these ones can and should have consciousness of sins, because they are not abiding in Christ at all.

But those who are humble enough to be honest, who confess their sins and forsake them, who trust in the Blood of Jesus as their sacrifice, these are the ones whose lawless deeds God remembers no more. And if God remembers them no more – past, present, or future – neither should anyone else.

Biblical Cure for Sin Consciousness

Let's examine this doctrine through Romans 5:12-17: *"Wherefore, as by one man sin entered into the word, and death by sin; and so, death passed upon all men, for that all have sinned: (For until the law sin was in the world: but sin is not imputed when there is no law. Nevertheless, death reigned from Adam to Moses, even over them that had not sinned after the similitude of Adam's transgression, who is the figure of him that was to come. But not as the offence, so also is the free gift. For if through the offense of one many be dead, much more of the grace of God, and the gift by grace, which is by one man, Jesus Christ, hath abounded unto many. And not as it was by one that sinned, so is the gift: for the judgment was by one to condemnation, but the gift is of many offences unto justification. For if by one man's offence death reigned by one; much more they which received abundance of grace and of the gift of righteousness shall reign in life by one, Jesus Christ".*

Notice Paul clearly expresses the failure of Man's works to measure up to the standard of God's righteousness, no matter how good they are. The word "entered" is the Greek word *elserchomai*. It means a foreign object, something that came from the outside inward.

The Apostle James declared openly in James 1:13-17: *"Let no man say when he is tempted, I am tempted of God: for*

God cannot be tempted with evil, neither tempteth he any man: But every man is tempted, when he is drawn away of his own lust, and enticed. Then when lust hath conceived, it bringeth forth sin: and sin, when it is finished, bringeth forth death. Do not err, my beloved brethren. Every good gift and every perfect gift is from above, and cometh down from the Father of lights, with whom is no variableness, neither shadow of turnin"g.

The word sin is not a creation of God, as you see in Genesis chapters 1 and 2, where through one man, sin entered the world. ("World" in Greek means activities or things) God doesn't inspire or allow sin or count sin or its commission, but sin exists as a function of Man's will. From the beginning of creation, God gave Man the freedom to choose what he wants to be, what he wants to do, and how he wants to act. Man is a free moral agent with desire.

When Adam made the choice to sin, God didn't stop him because Adam had a right to choose, but Adam could not control the outcome of his choice. God, in His infinite mercy, came as a man to rescue Man from the consequences of Man's actions (Romans 6:23). Jesus rescued Man by paying Man's death (Hebrews 2:9).

Jesus told us in John 5, *"Verily, verily I say unto you, He that heareth my word, and believeth on him that sent me, hath everlasting life, and shall not come into condemnation; but is passed from death unto life."* (John 5:24). Jesus said believers would not come into condemnation, so if that is God's portion for the believers, why does a believer's heart condemn him? The problem is that many believers have been taught an incorrect doctrine of sanctification and righteousness. I was a victim of that too. God's prescription for sin is not sinless-ness or sinless perfection. Rather,

God's prescription for sin and its consciousness is righteousness.

Justify Justified, Righteous

Romans 3:20-27 reads, *"Therefore by the deeds of the law there shall no flesh be justified in his sight: for by the law is the knowledge of sin. But now the righteous of God without the law is manifested, being witnessed by the law and the prophets; Even the righteousness of God which is by faith of Jesus Christ unto all and upon all them that believe: for there is no difference: for all have sinned, and come short the glory of God; Being justified freely by his grace through the redemption that is in Christ Jesus: Whom God hath set forth to be a propitiation through faith in his blood, to declare his righteousness for the remission of sins that are past, through the forbearance of God; To declare, I say, at this time his righteousness: that he might be just, and the justifier of him who believeth in Jesus. Where is boasting then? It is excluded. By what law? of works? Nay: but by the law of faith".*

Pay attention to the use of the words "justify," "justified," and "righteousness" in the Scriptures above. The discussion was about sin. Sin means something that is wrong, and that has not changed since Genesis.

The word "justified" is the Greek word *dikaioo*. It is used in court when there is a judicial approval of someone or something, when the judge takes your side. When a charge is brought against you before a judge, and the judge declares in your favor, that means he has justified you. The judge now defends you without defending you, even though you have a lawyer. By saying "you are not guilty as charged," he has defended you and has come to your aid.

The word "justify" means to come to another's aid; to approve or to declare someone as upright or as right. Paul used it in Romans 5:1. *"Therefore being justified by faith, we have peace with God through our Lord Jesus Christ.".* You were approved because of faith. You are also justified by His blood. The word, "peace" in Romans 5:1 is *eirene* in the Greek, which means union with God resulting from justification. We are united with God. It's faith in what He has done that justifies.

Back to the word *dikaioo*. It means you were justified on legal terms, but the terms were not your terms. It was the third party that brought about that justification. Notice that you are justified by a third party: His grace through His blood (Romans 5:1). The law of man is not justified by works. A third party came to your aid or stood for you, and because of that third party, you are declared approved of God. Romans 4:25 reads, *"Who was delivered for our offences and raised again for our justification.".*

Titus 3:7 says, *"having been justified."* This phrase is one word in the Greek: *diakiothentes*, which implies you are being justified and will always be justified. Justification is in the present, continuing tense. Romans 5:17 says, *"Much more they which receive abundance of grace and of the gift of righteousness shall reign in life by one, Jesus Christ.".* The word "gift" in this verse is the Greek word *dorea*, meaning it's free. There is no condition attached. It is another word for benevolence. The gift of righteousness is free and has no condition attached to it.

Then we have the word "righteousness," which is the Greek word *dikaiosune*, meaning "you are right." *Dikaioo* relates to the act; *dikaiosune* relates to the state. Being justified by faith and justified by grace, the person God did justify is now justified. He now has righteousness. Based on what Christ has done, he acquires a state or a status.

Dikaiosune means a state and status. In the Bible, *dikaiosune* is used exclusively for God. Since He is the judge of all. He is righteous; whatever He says or does is right. We only know what is right or wrong from what God says, so God is called Just because he is God.

Dikaiosune in Greek has the same meaning as the Hebrew *tsedaqah* – a state of being proper or a state of being right, usually translated as "for righteousness." It is the word used in Genesis 5:6. *Misphat* in Hebrew is to do justice, to do right. It is the same word in Greek, which means to justify, to treat as proper, to deal with as right.

Abraham believed God, and it was counted to him as *dikaiosune.* He is seen as someone who will do right; hence, God's statement in Genesis 18:19 was in line with what He has declared him. The reason God could say "I know Abraham, he will do right" is because God himself is the only one who is right and has justified him. Abraham entered a state where he was said to do right, But Before he was in this state, he had been acquired and justified. How was he justified? In Genesis 18:19 God was not talking about Abraham's conduct but Abraham's faith. So, righteousness is for one who has done rightly.

Romans 3:25 reads, *"Whom God hath set forth to be a propitiation through faith in his blood, to declare his righteousness for the remission of sins that are past, through the forbearance of God".* Notice how Paul builds his case. In verse 24, he says *"being justified freely by his grace through the redemption that is in Christ Jesus."* Being justified how? Freely! Who is going to justify him? God. And He is doing it without attaching conditions – freely by His grace. There must be a legal reason for what He is doing. So, He now says *"through the redemption that is in Christ."*

Paul is establishing God's conduct as proper. God did not just act. He had a legal basis. *"To declare, I say at this time his righteousness: that he might be just, and the justifier of him which believeth in Jesus."* (Romans 3:26). God displayed His nature of always doing right. What is God's justification for justifying you? You can see clearly on a legal basis that what God did was right. So, justification is not a function of feeling; it is a legal issue. God has done these things on perfectly legal grounds.

Righteousness is not forgiveness. It is also not pardon. It means you have been declared right; you have no wrong ever in you. In the eyes of God, you are as right and holy as though you have never sinned before. How did God do it? It is not based on what the person did; it was a third-party action that justified the man.

Romans 4:5 reads *"But to him that worketh not, but believeth on him that justifieth the ungodly, his faith is counted for righteousness.".* The word "Justifieth" is the Greek word *dikaion*. It's another tense of the word *dikaiosune*, used here for a state of being perfect. That is, the man is judicially declared as perfect. Remember the context is a discourse on Abraham; so, let me explain the word ungodly.

Abraham was an ungodly man when God called him. The word "ungodly" is the Greek word *asebes*, used for criminal, wicked, morally bankrupt people – those who go to Hell. That was what Abraham was in his conduct, yet God used a legal way to declare him righteous, acquitting him perfectly. So, righteousness does not come from a man. It's a gift. The Scripture says when something is of works, it's not a gift but a debt. But when something is of grace, it is not a reward for good works.

Many of us grew up with the wrong understanding that righteousness is a reward for consistent church attendance and good conduct. This is a wrong mentality. God justified the ungodly. Again, how does God justify the ungodly? Romans 5:6 reads, *"For when we were yet without strength, in due time Christ died for the ungodly."*

Christ died for the ungodly. That's the basis on which God *dikaisune* or *dikaioo* (justifieth) the sinner. The wages of sin is death. Someone paid for it, and it will not be held against the sinner again. Christ died for the wicked. He did not die out of pity, but rather it was a demonstration of His love. So, righteousness is on very equitable terms. Romans 5:8 reads, *"But God commendeth his love towards us, in that, while we were yet sinners, Christ died for us"*

The word "sinners' is used for rebels. So, Jesus, the third party, died to declare rebels right. Romans 8:31-32 declares, *"What shall we then say to these things? If God be for us, who can be against us? He that spared not his own Son, but delivered him up for us all, how shall he not with him also freely give us all things?"*

The word 'if' is used for 'since,' or as a rhetorical question, in Romans. "Since God be for us." "Be for us" is the Greek word *dikaioo* (Justified), so the verse can be read as: Since God has justified you, what can stand against you?

You are only a beneficiary of the justification – you are not a party. God's attitude toward sinners is favor. God does not use sin; He does not tempt with sin; and He does not overlook sin. He favors the sinner on perfect legal grounds. How? By the death of His Son Jesus.

The favor a man enjoys at the point he receives Jesus is the favor he enjoys forever, because the sacrifice is once and forever. Right actions are good, but right actions don't justify. Nothing about a man is right. David even knew better in the Old Testament. He said, *"If thou, LORD, shouldest mark iniquities, O Lord, who shall stand?"* (Psalms 130:3).

Satan The Accuser and His Accusation

The word "accuse" is used thirty times in the Bible. It is from the Greek word *diabolos,* also used for Satan, or devil. It is related to the word "diabolical," which means prone to slander or being slanderous. It refers to someone that makes a charge to bring down (destroy) others. Once in the Bible, the word *diabolos* was used in reference to demons. *Diabolos* literally means a slanderer or a deceiver or a false accuser. It is also used as a metaphor for a man that opposes the cause of God, a man that sides with the devil or acts the part of Satan.

To accuse, therefore, is to lay blame on someone with the intention of having him sentenced to punishment, to charge someone with a fault or offence, or to charge with an offence judicially or by public process. The intention of accusation is to destroy someone. All these describe the exact nature of Satan. Satan, which means slanderer, is the accuser of the brethren. That is his job. Titus 2:3 and 2 Timothy 3:3 point to this fact. Revelation 12:10 declares, *"And I heard a loud voice saying in heaven, Now is come salvation, and strength, and the kingdom of our God, and the power of his Christ: for the accuser of our brethren is cast down, which accused them before our God day and night".*

The voice was referring to Christ's triumph through His resurrection, when he defeated the accuser, principalities, and powers. Colossians 2:15 reads, *"And having spoiled all principalities and powers, he made a shew of them openly, triumphing over them in it."* He disarmed them and took them captive. The next thing Paul says is *"let no man therefore judge you."* The accuser of the brethren has been disarmed and spoiled; no man should therefore judge you. Lots of believers think and act as though Satan has not been defeated. They ascribe to the devil what he does not possess.

Some believers cry in prayers and even beg demons to leave them alone. The assumption is that demons have tremendous powers, so believers cannot really face them. This is the lie Satan wants you to believe, but Satan has no such power over the believer! The day Jesus was raised from death, He triumphed over sin and death. The last Adam had undone the works of the first Adam. Jesus has taken His position as the resurrected Lord over His Church. Satan cannot undo what Jesus has done. Jesus has purified earth by His sacrifice of Himself.

It is also important, to note that the word "accuse" is never used by the judge but rather by the opponent. In Greek, "accuse" or "accuser" is *kaegoros*, meaning to accuse someone with the intention of condemning him, it also means a prosecutor. A prosecutor in court is not the judge. He can prosecute but has no authority to condemn. *Kaegoros*, which literally means accuser, is a name given to the devil by the rabbis. It conveys the meaning of verbal attacks or verbal assaults. It is used symbolically as something that hits like a bullet. Accusation always comes in words.

Jesus used the Greek word *kaegoros* several times in the Gospel, and it was also used about Jesus in relation to the Jews' response to His ministry while on earth. Let's look at some scriptural references. Bear with me. I must give you scriptural references and quotes to help you understand from a Biblical point of view. If I fail to provide these scriptural backings, then I'm only speaking psychology and head knowledge.

Luke 6:6-7 reads, *"And it came to pass also on another sabbath, that he entered into the synagogue and taught: and there was a man whose right hand was withered. And the scribes and Pharisees watched him, whether he would heal on the sabbath day; that they might find an accusation against him".*

These scriptures reference the same situation. The scribes and Pharisees sought means to accuse Jesus. They thought to provoke him to do what would go against their interpretation of the law of the Sabbath, to find an occasion of launching a verbal attack against Him.

The Greek word *kaegoros* was used in all three versions of the story. It was also used in the book of Luke. *"And they began to accuse him, saying We found this fellow perverting the nation, and forbidding to give tribute to Ceasar, saying that he himself is Christ a King."* (Luke 23:2). In Pilate's response to them, he said, *"Ye have brought this man unto me, as one that perverteth the people: and, behold I, having examined him before you, have found no fault in this man touching those things whereof ye accuse him."* (Luke 23:14).

The leaders of the people – the chief priests and the leaders of the Jews – brought these verbal assaults against Jesus before Pilate, who was the Roman governor in Israel at the time. They thought to pitch Him against the Roman authority in order have Him punished by death.

All the devil was after was to get Jesus out of his way. These religious leaders were just being used by evil spirits. After Satan tempted Jesus in the wilderness, the Bible says he left Him for a while. *"And when the devil had ended all the temptation, he departed from him for a season."* (Luke 4:13). Satan came back in the skin of Pharisees and Sadducees and lawyers and as many of the leaders that could make themselves available to him to be influenced. They were all his mouthpiece, throwing accusations against Jesus at every opportunity.

Jesus used *kategoros* in connection to Israel's response to the Law of Moses. John 5:45-47, NASB reads, *"Do not think that I will accuse you before the Father; the one who accuses you is Moses, in whom you have set your hope. For if you believed Moses, you would believe Me, for he wrote about Me. But if you do not believe his writings, how will you believe My words?"*

Jesus did not mean Moses as a person was their accuser, of course not. He did not mean that Moses was there with God accusing them. That would be a misrepresentation of what He was saying.

There is no other scripture that holds that view in the New Testament. Also, Moses did not play the role of Satan at any time. He, as a person, was certainly not the accuser of the Jews. We can only understand this fully when we take a closer look at Jesus' meaning.

We must understand what he meant by "Moses" in that Scripture. "Moses" was used in place of "the law." Moses signified the law. Jesus was not talking about the person of

Moses but was referring to the writings of Moses, the Law of Moses. He was saying the Law of Moses brings a legal case against them before God. In other words, Jesus was saying that the Law of Moses was their accuser. The writings of Moses were against them because they did not believe nor obey what Moses wrote.

The Law of Moses held them guilty for not believing what was written in the law. Jesus is not a fault-finder. He is not looking for errors in people's lives to condemn them. He did not come to run a ministry of condemnation on earth, and He still does not run one. Jesus came to a world that was condemned by sin to set it free from the judgment of death. Jesus told His audience that the law that they trusted so much and had tried to keep was against them because they did not obey it. Had they harkened to the writings of Moses, they would have known and received Jesus.

Recall the other meaning of the word "accuse" is to prosecute. In other words, Jesus was saying that the law of Moses prosecutes them before God because they do not fulfill what it says. Jesus went on to explain that Moses wrote about Him, so it is explicit that He was talking about the writings of Moses, not the person of Moses. If they had believed the writings of Moses, they would have believed Jesus. That they did not believe Him was proof that they did not believe the writings of Moses. So, the Law of Moses was their accuser. In Jesus' words, the entire writing of Moses was about Him. Without Him, there would be no Moses (the Mosaic Law). Jesus was the reason for the Mosaic Law, so Christ was the message.

Accusations are always in words, and they hit like bullets. They are never meant to give you any chance to reason them out. They are spoken with a note of finality to cast judgment on you. Your accusers do not expect you to respond and explain yourself.

Their words are intended to spell final judgment for you. Jesus experienced a lot of accusations while on earth but refused to respond. Matthew 27:12-14 reads, *"And when he was accused of the chief priests and elders, he answered nothing. Then said Pilate unto him, Hearest thou not how many things they witness against thee? And he answered him to never a word; insomuch that the governor marveled greatly"*.

Words were spoken stoutly against Jesus before Pilate. The leaders verbally assaulted Him with many words, but He did not answer a word against His accusers. Jesus did not explain Himself nor throw accusation on them to prove them wrong or straighten out their argument. Jesus was such a disciplined man; He understood the power of words.

Also, there are false accusations and there are accusations that are not necessarily false. When they accused Jesus of perverting the people, it was false. Jesus did not pervert anybody in deeds or words. Pilate soon found out that they lied, but although Jesus knew they were lying against Him, He did not answer them a word.

Peter talked about people being falsely accused saying. *"Having a good conscience; that, whereas they speak evil of you, as of evildoers, they may be ashamed that they falsely accuse your good conversation in Christ. For it is better if the will of God be so, that ye suffer for well doing, than for evil doing. For Christ also hath once suffered for sins, the just for the unjust, that he might bring us to God, being put to death in the flesh, but quickened by the Spirit"*. (1 Peter 3:16-18)

This shows us a pattern of being falsely accused. Pilate acceded to that fact when he said he found in Jesus no cause for death. 1 Peter 2:23 reads, *"And he said unto them the third time, Why, what evil hath he done? I have found no cause of death in him: I will therefore chastise him and let him go."* (Luke 23:22). Jesus was falsely assaulted with words, but He did not answer. He was within the will of God not to answer His accusers. The Bible says when Jesus was reviled, He reviled not.

Jesus knew the purpose of His coming. He was not guilty of what he was accused of, but someone else was guilty. He was bearing our guilt upon Himself, so He threatened not. If Jesus defended Himself, we would be the losers! We are the beneficiaries of His suffering. He committed Himself to the will of the Father, the righteous Judge.

In the same way Jesus responded when accused falsely, He did not say we should defend ourselves when we are falsely accused by the devil. Jesus died on the cross so that He would receive our accusations, false or guilty, and in so doing, receive our punishment and free us from eternal judgment. He did that to secure our salvation. Not all accusations are false, but every accusation has one objective: to bring condemnation.

The Case of the Woman Caught in Adultery

John 8:3-11 tell of the story of this woman. It reads, *"And the scribes and Pharisees brought unto him a woman taken in adultery; and when they had set her in the midst, They say unto him, Master, this woman was taken in adultery, in the very act. Now Moses in the law commanded us, that such should be stoned: but what sayest thou? This they said, tempting him, that they might have to accuse him. But Jesus stooped down, and with his finger wrote on the ground, as though he heard them not. So when they continued asking him, he lifted up himself and said unto them, He that is without sin among you, let him first cast a stone at her. And again he stooped down, and wrote on the ground. And they which heard it, being convicted by their own conscience, went out one by one, beginning at the eldest, even unto the last: and Jesus was left alone, and the woman standing in the midst. When Jesus had lifted up himself, and saw none but the woman, he said unto her, Woman, where are those thine accusers? hath no man condemned thee? She said, No man, Lord. And Jesus said unto her, Neither do I condemn thee: go, and sin no more".*

This woman was not falsely accused. She was caught in the very act of adultery. The scribes and Pharisees are Moses' employees, so to speak. They were the defenders of the Mosaic law. They knew the Torah and interpreted the law. Pharisees knew the laws of Moses, the Psalms, and the Major Prophets by heart. One could not qualify as a Pharisee until he knew all of this.

So, these were not ordinary people. They did not need to consult the Torah to know the exact punishment this woman deserved. They were like the walking law. To authenticate and give legal backing and establish a doctrinal case against this woman before Jesus, they quoted from the law. There was an actual sin, and she was caught right in it. There was core evidence against her, and there was a law backing her execution. Jesus was called a rabbi, so they provided a legal standing for her case before Jesus to nail the woman, so that she could be sentenced.

This woman was already condemned to death by stoning based on the law, but someone without sin would have to enact the punishment on her. She was guilty by the Law of Moses. Her accusers were not ordinary people; they were Doctors of the Law. They referenced Deuteronomy 20:10 and Deuteronomy 22:21 to back up their accusation. The people accusing this woman did not just throw stones at people. They had hard facts on this woman's case, but they had to back it up with what the law said. Without the law, no act is a sin. For it to be a sin, they must show the position of law.

The Bible defines sin as the transgression of the law. 1John 3:4 reads, *"Whosoever committeth sin transgresseth also the law: for sin is the transgression of the law."* Unless your action transgressed the Law of Moses, you did not sin. This woman was certainly not falsely accused. There was a guilty verdict on her head.

Why didn't they punish the woman according to their law since she was caught in the very act? They were not just after that woman. They knew the situation of the law and what the law prescribed in dealing with the case of adultery. They didn't need to bring her to Jesus. Why did they bring this woman to Jesus? These are accusers. They accused the woman and brought her to Jesus in order to use her case to accuse Jesus of breaking the Law of Moses should He not tell them to stone her.

There were holes in their case, though, because the position of the law was that both participants in the sin should be brought to justice, but they brought only the woman and left the man. Secondly, the woman that should be punished by stoning like this must have been betrothed to someone, but that woman was not. This was a case of adultery or even fornication. They faulted the law by not considering these two positions of the law first. These people desperately wanted to find something to accuse Jesus of; it was a trap they were setting for Jesus.

They knew Jesus would not condemn that woman. They never saw or heard him condemn anybody, so they thought Jesus would tell them the woman was not guilty, and they could find cause to accuse Him of breaching the Law of Moses. But if Jesus passed a verdict of condemnation on her, they could say He did not show her mercy. Therefore, He was not the Christ, and Israel should not believe in Him. Wow!! What a well-crafted strategy against Jesus Christ.

A fundamental aspect of messiahship was to pardon sin, so if Jesus failed to do that, He could not be the Messiah. They were out to find fault with both Jesus and the woman. But Jesus acted as though He did not hear them. He stooped down and wrote on the ground with His finger. He just ignored them, but they thought they had gotten Him in a corner and continued to ask Him. Jesus then lifted Himself and told them that any one of them that was without sin, let him cast the stone, and He again stooped down and wrote with His finger on the ground.

They understood from the writing of Isaiah that there was no one righteous man. For Isaiah said *"Who hath declared from the beginning, that we may know? and before time, that we may say, He is righteous? yea, there is none that sheweth, yea, there is none that declareth, yea, there is none that heareth your words."* (Isaiah 41:26). Again, Isaiah said, *"All we like sheep have gone astray; we have turned everyone to his own way; and the LORD hath laid on him the iniquity of us all."* (Isaiah 53:6). With these and many other writings in the Law of Moses, it was obvious that none of them could cast a stone against that woman.

The only person that has the righteousness to judge or condemn another person is the Person that has no sin. So, Jesus asked any one of them that was in a position to condemn that woman to be the first to cast the stone against her. They were all convicted by their conscience and walked away one by one, beginning from the oldest to the youngest.

They could accuse, but they couldn't condemn Her. They had to take Her to Pilate, who had the civil authority to condemn. The accuser doesn't condemn, all he does is accuse. The only person qualified to condemn this woman was Jesus. He was the only one without sin. Had Jesus not known the law, He would not have gotten out of that.

When you come before the court, it is the law that will either condemn you or set you free. Every lawyer in the courtroom will cite the law. They would quote from the law and previous judgments to argue their case, but only the judge has the power to pronounce a guilty or not guilty verdict.

Only the judge will issue the sentence according to his knowledge of the law. He could also temper justice with mercy. The lawyers and the accusers do not decide the sentence. The judge has the prerogative to do so. You are not judged and sentenced based on people's feelings or bias; you are judged by law. You can feel emotional in the courtroom and weep, but it won't change the position of the law.

In fact, in some cases, your show of emotions through tears, could put you in more trouble in the courtroom because the law is not subject to your emotions. You can beg the judge, or your loved ones can join in begging and weeping in the court. Even all the people in the court can join in begging the judge, but all of that won't change anything.

The judge doesn't go by his emotions; he goes by the law. No matter the level of empathy the judge may have towards you, he will judge the case on its merit. There is no sentiment in the court room, it's justice that matters. Therefore, you must understand the legality of your redemption through Christ. If you do not understand the legality of redemption, you will never stay free. You will never be sure of anything until you know that you were saved based on justice that was meted on Christ.

Satan will always seek to push you into doubt over the legality of your redemption. That is how he can make you shift from your standing in faith into feelings. He wants to drive you with guilt until you lose your grounding of faith and start to doubt your salvation in Christ.

When Satan came against Jesus to tempt Him in Matthew 4, he did not expect to lose. There would be no need for the temptation if he knew he would lose the case. The temptation happened after Jesus' baptism in water by John, in which a voice from heaven declared Jesus His beloved Son, in whom He is well pleased, ending it by saying "hear ye him."

The first thing Satan did was to throw a dart at Jesus' identity, as he did with Eve in the Garden of Eden. He tried to cause Jesus to doubt His identity and to feel God neglected Him. He tried to challenge His power and asked Him to command stones to turn in to bread to prove He was the Son of God.

It's not that Jesus could not have commanded stones into bread, but if He did, He would have obeyed Satan, not God. If Jesus wanted bread, He needed to hear from God, not Satan. Jesus was hungry when Satan came, having been fasting for 40 days. Satan struck at the time that Jesus could fall, at the point of His need.

Jesus told Satan that if He needed bread, He would get it from God speaking to Him. He told him that He lives by the words that proceed from the mouth of God. In another attack, Satan began to quote from the Scripture to validate his temptation. Satan is always on a legal ground to bring accusation. Satan does not guess his way around people, he presents facts. That is why your knowledge of the Word of God must be deep and precise (Philemon 1:6).

The scribes and Pharisees did not have a frivolous accusation against this woman. She was caught in the very act. It was not hearsay or a suspicion. They had hard core evidence. They did not think that they would lose that case. To them, the judgment was sure and the verdict certain.

When Satan accuses you, he presents you with the facts. If he says you stole, he will cause you to see the picture of how and when it happened. He will not guess about the accusation. Even you yourself know that what he is saying did happen; that is why Satan's accusations torment people and fill them with guilt.

The scribes and Pharisees laid out the legal ground for the condemnation of this woman. They were not in doubt of the outcome. What the scribes and Pharisees did not know, however, was that they were standing right before a higher law. They were asking the Chief Justice in heaven and on earth the final say about the law to condemn that woman. They did not consider that He had the prerogative to temper justice with mercy.

When Jesus lifted Himself up and found that they had gone, He asked the woman, "Woman, where are those your accusers?" and she said they all have gone, Jesus said unto her, neither do I condemn thee: go and sin no more." Jesus identified the scribes and Pharisees that brought her as accusers. But they did not have the power to condemn her. Once she called Jesus "Lord," she received mercy from God.

Jesus called her "woman." He did not call her prostitute. He called her woman. To the accuser, she was an adulteress, a prostitute, but Jesus identified her by who she was, not what she did. He called her "woman." Jesus, who had the power to condemn her, chose not to condemn. He told her to go and sin no more.

In Jesus' words, you must be without sin to condemn anybody, or else you must stay mute. You have no business talking about another man's sin. Even if you have evidence against others, if you are with sin, your evidence against the accused does not put you in the position to judge another human being.

Repentance is simply a change of one's mind.

This woman's accusers left her alone. They could not condemn her because they were not sin-free. Their conscience pricked them, and they left one by one. Accusation does not mean condemnation, though that is its target. That you are accused, falsely or otherwise, doesn't mean you are condemned.

The Gift of "No Condemnation"

Jesus asked this woman if she was condemned by any of her accusers, but she answered, "No one my Lord." When she called him Lord, she submitted to His Lordship. She would be bound by whatever verdict Jesus gave. You do not call Jesus Lord and get sentenced to death or condemned. When you call and recognize Jesus as your Lord, you get salvation. Saul of Tarsus called Him "Lord" when he was confronted by Jesus on the road to Damascus on a murderous mission (Acts 9). Jesus confronted Saul to stop him from his wicked act, but when he asked, "Who are you Lord," it was an admission of Jesus' authority.

Do you realize that the light that shone on him was brighter than the sun that shone in his path? It was so bright that it knocked him down from his horse and blinded him. Saul of Tarsus was a smart man. He called Him Lord first before he tried to know who He was that was talking to him from the light. When the woman called him "Lord," it was her submission to the mercy of God.

Jesus said to her, "neither do I condemn you." What Jesus gave this woman was the gift of "no condemnation." She did not deserve it. She deserved death by stoning, according to her deeds. She received a gift, not a payment. Jesus gave her "no condemnation." She was acquitted and discharged in the face of hard evidence. The grace of God set her free irrespective of the claims against her.

The Gift of righteousness precedes Repentance.

The gift of 'no condemnation' is called righteousness. There is something else I want you to see here. When this woman stood before Jesus, she did not repent for what she did. She did not tell Jesus that she was sorry for her actions, even when the accusers had all left and she stood before Jesus alone. She was not sorry for her actions and gave no promise that she would not do it again. All she did was to call him Lord. When she did that, she walked away a free woman. Her accusers could not come back to judge her. She had been made free by the highest Judge. No one could touch her again. In fact, there was no reference to that matter anymore in the Gospels.

This event happened before Jesus went to the cross and died for us. The gift of righteousness (no condemnation) was given to this woman before repentance. This is so because it is the gift of righteousness that helps you to repent. Repentance is a change of mind. Until you receive the life of Christ, you have no authority over your mind.

Your mind rules you until your spirit is recreated in Christ. So, the gift of righteousness precedes repentance. The Bible says it's God's goodness that leads to repentance. Romans 4:5 reads, *"Or despisest thou the riches of his goodness and forbearance and longsuffering; not knowing that the goodness of God leadeth thee to repentance."* You are to believe in Him who justifies the ungodly. That's how it works. You believe first, and God will give you the gift of "no condemnation." Righte-ousness removes timidity; it makes you bold.

No Enemy can stand as a threat before a believer that knows his rights in the kingdom of God. When you receive the words of God, those words "reboot" your life for maximum productivity.

Your mind rules you
Until your spirit is recreated in Christ.

Religion feeds sin and brings out the strength of sin consciousness. Righteousness and justification are the same thing. When you are justified, you are made righteous. It has nothing to do with what you did or what you did not do. The woman's works were not considered when Jesus set her free. She would not be set free if her works were considered. She was caught in the very act of adultery! But she believes the word of Jesus.

What faith in the Lordship of Jesus accomplishes for you, your righteous works or good deeds won't provide. You cannot work out spiritual things any other way but by faith in Christ Jesus, and faith only receives what Grace has provided.

Accusation Is Not Positive

Accusation is not for correction; it brings condemnation. The accuser does not come up with positive things about you; he brings negative things. But for him to successfully accuse you, he must be without sin.

Anyone that is sinful has no right to condemn you. He must stop at accusation. You can see why you should not give Satan any room in your life. Satan is the accuser of the brethren, but he cannot go beyond accusation. All he has are verbal accusations; he cannot condemn because there is sin in him. He must be sin-free to judge anybody. Satan is sinful. He is the president and founder of sin. He lacks the legal and moral grounds to condemn anybody. When you sin, you do not sin against Satan. Satan has no law for anybody to breach. He is lawless. He only took advantage of the Law of Moses to bring men into the condemnation of sin.

You need to grasp this truth in order to experience your true freedom in Christ Jesus. You do not sin against Satan. You sinned against God. So, in the first place, Satan has no business accusing you. He has no legal jurisdiction over a believer that sins. All the demands for sin were paid by Jesus on the Cross. That brought us into the family of God. Satan has been kicked out. When you sin, you do so within the confinement of the family. It is a family matter. God is the head of this family, and only He can settle the matter of sin.

The beauty of this is that God has settled all sin problems in Christ. He settled everything over two thousand years ago. God is not interested in the sin issue anymore. He's made the blood of Jesus the propitiation for sin. Satan can do nothing about this. The blood of Jesus is a judge against him.

All Satan does is throw verbal assaults. He reminds you of your many wrong doings of the past. He uses things you did years ago to confront your future. He does not even know what your future holds. He relies on your past and present to throw accusation against you.

He tries to confront your claim of righteousness by throwing darts into your mind, reminding you what you did wrong. That is where the battle is, in the mind, and you need the Word of God to take authority over your mind. Joyce Meyer calls it the "battlefield of the mind."

2 Corinthians 10:3-5 reads, *"For though we walk in the flesh, we do not war after the flesh: (For the weapons of our warfare are not carnal, but mighty through God to the pulling down strong holds;) Casting down imaginations, and every high thing that exalteth itself against the knowledge of God, and bringing into capacity every thought to the obedience of Christ."*

We are not fighting flesh and blood. Our weapon is not carnal. We do not fight with guns and bullets. We fight with words! The stronghold of the enemy is not some demonic structure erected somewhere. Principalities do not rule in some families or communities.

Strongholds are thoughts and imaginations that are contrary to the provision of redemption. Satan assaults us with words. He tries to dominate our minds with words that interpret our natural life and environment. We'll only overcome him with the word of redemption. When he throws those negative words on, trash them and take authority of the thoughts or doubts and unbelief that he brings against you. Remind yourself of what the Word of God says about you.

Satan is more afraid of your knowledge of the Word of God in you, and your consciousness of your spiritual rights than he is about your 40 days of prayer and fasting.

That is the battle. It is fought with the words, and it is a continual one. He is an accuser; words are his tools of operation. You must subject every word to the authority of Christ. Satan brings words before us and shows us how unqualified and unfit we are to claim righteousness.

He tries to drive us to the point of guilt until we are depressed. Satan's attack gets at you because you are untrained, unskilled in the word of righteousness. When your conscience is not trained in the Word of God, Satan uses your conscience to deal with you. Your conscience, if untrained in the knowledge of God, can be a source of weakness in your life. Satan will keep you on the path of condemnation all the time.

CHAPTER 10

THE REVELATION OF
THE CROSS

A brand-new spiritual atmosphere came to the earth after the resurrection of Christ. The cross of Jesus was designed to establish a new spiritual benchmark. It was preordained from the foundation of the world as a means of escape from sin and its corruption.

There are resources and levels of relationship with God now available to men after the cross that were not there before the cross. No man had the ability to stand before God without a sense of guilt, condemnation, inferiority, and sin consciousness. But after the cross, the basis of relationship with God changed, and the born-again man had access to God's unsearchable riches.

Everything is now based on the unearned, underserved, unmerited favor of God and not our performance. When the death certificate of the Testator was produced and the triumph of His reign over death in resurrection was announced, Christ's riches, legacies, and redemption treasures were transferred to us.

We now reign along with Him. There are unimaginable levels of glory released for the dominion and comfort of the man in Christ. But due to ignorance of these realities through wrong teachings, many believers are still living their lives as if Jesus did not complete a perfect job in His death, burial, and resurrection as our substitutionary sacrifice.

But it is on record that Hebrews 10:12,14 reads, *"This man, after he had offered one sacrifice for sins forever, sat down on the right hand of God; ...For by the offering he hath perfected forever them that are sanctified."*. This is the announcement of a perfect job, well done and totally completed on Man's behalf, for all time and all eternity.

The Cross Demarcates the Old from the New Testament.

The cross of Jesus Christ changed everything as it relates to the manner of life that existed before the death of Jesus, and this is the crux of the matter in Christianity that many fails to realize. The difference between the Old and New Testament is the cross. Matthew 26:28 reads, *"For this is my blood of the new testament, which is shed for many for the remission of sins."*

The cross is Satan's greatest nightmare but, mercifully, the believer's advantage. The message of grace is the message that reveals what the cross (the death, burial, and resurrection of Jesus) accomplished for us. Hebrews 2:14-15 reads, *"Forasmuch then as the children are partakers of flesh and blood, He also himself likewise took part of the same; that through death he might destroy him that had the power of death, that is, the devil; and deliver them who through fear of death were all their lifetime subject to bondage."*

Everything changed because of the cross. Satan practically lost everything by reason of the cross. His hope today is only kindled by the ignorance of believers and mere men. If the message of the cross and its power is hidden, Man becomes a victim all over again. 2 Corinthians 4:3-4 *boldly declares; "But if our gospel be hid, it is hid to them that are lost: In whom the god of this world hath blinded the minds of them which believe not, lest the light of the glorious gospel of Christ, who is the image of God, should shine unto them."*

1 Corinthians 1:18 also clearly stated the importance of the cross, saying, *"For the preaching of the cross is to them that perish foolishness; but unto us which are saved it is the power of God.".* The cross reveals the depth of the nature of the love of God and His heart and mind towards Man. We cannot appreciate God's nature or His eternal purpose without the revelation of the cross. Many people are going through life missing out on God's best for them because they lack this understanding due to their spiritual state.

The Difference between the Old and New Testament is the Cross.

The Cross was the hardest teaching of Jesus to be understood by His disciples. It was used by the Jews to show a person who was a societal reject, one who was denied. It was a punishment for first degree criminals like Barabbas. (*See* Mathew 27:16-17). Jesus was not a criminal, but He was to die the death of a criminal, as was written before time. The chief priest during the time of Jesus' death also prophesied unknowingly about the same. (*See* John 11:49-52).

The death Jesus died was not for Him but for Man. It was not His cross, but He bore it for Mankind, for you and I. When Jesus began to tell his disciples about how the kingdom was to come, they could not understand because their minds were unable to comprehend what he was saying. *"From that time forth began Jesus to shew unto his disciples, how that he must go unto Jerusalem, and suffer many things of the elders and chief priests and scribes, and be killed, and be raised again the third day. Then Peter took him, and began to rebuke him, saying, Be it far from thee, Lord: this shall not be unto thee. But he turned, and said unto Peter, Get thee behind me, Satan: thou art an offence unto me: for thou savourest not the things that be of God, but those that be of men." Matthew 16:21-23*

The word 'SAVOUREST' was used to show what was of interest to Peter. Jesus was not calling Peter the devil but was pointing to the interest of Satan in the material things of the world. Jesus, by His response, lets us know that the kingdom of God is not in material things or the natural riches of this earth. The disciples and all those that heard Jesus could not have understood Him. They understood kingdom, authority, and power in things, so Jesus' preaching of the cross was foolishness to them.

The Power of the Message of the Cross

The revelation of the cross will be seen in that which the Spirit revealed concerning His death: Jesus' three days and nights in Hades, His resurrection, ascension, and exaltation to the right hand of the Father. The resurrection is the cap of perfection to all that Jesus accomplished. This is the show of God's almighty power alone to save. Romans 1:16 reads, *"For I am not ashamed of the gospel of Christ: for it is the power of God unto salvation to everyone that believeth; to the Jew first, and also to the Greek."*

Men are persuaded to believe; the gospel preached is God's wisdom to save. 1 Corinthians 1:21-24 *says, "For after that in the wisdom of God the world by wisdom knew not God, it pleased God by the foolishness of preaching to save them that believe. For the Jews require a sign, and the Greeks seek after wisdom: But we preach Christ crucified, unto the Jews a stumbling block, and unto the Greeks foolishness; But unto them which are called, both Jews and Greeks, Christ the power of God, and the wisdom of God."*

The major difference between the Old Testament and the New Testament is the manifestation of God in human form in the person of Jesus Christ. It was promised and prophesied about in the Old Testament. The cross reveals the desire of God, His intent and purpose, His wisdom and counsel. This power and wisdom of God is committed to our preaching of the love of God today.

Retiring from Works

The Cross has retired mankind from works of trying to please God or to gain redemption. The best thing you can do is give up on your own works.

Yes, give up. Quit. Don't even turn in a 2-weeks' notice. The business is going downhill already, and you are no longer needed as an employee. In fact, it went out of business about two thousand years ago when Jesus showed up. Retire from the broken-down religious establishment and come to a place of rest through Jesus' finished work on the cross. Start living in a place of rest. Enjoy the benefits of retirement – the finished work of the cross.

Jesus, through His death and resurrection, obtained for you what you are frustratingly trying to obtain for yourself. Too good to be true......and possibly even heretical.

Ok... Check out what the writer of Hebrew has to say about this: *"Therefore, let us fear if, while a promise remains of entering His rest, any one of you may seem to have come short of it. For indeed we have had good news preached to us, just as they also; but the word they heard did not profit them, because it was not united by faith in those who heard. For we who have believed enter that rest, just as He has said, 'AS I SWORE IN MY WRATH, THEY SHALL NOT ENTER MY REST,' although his works were finished from the foundation of the world." Hebrews 4:1-3 (NASB)*

I'll try to break this down quickly. The Hebrews were coming out of a system of law into the new covenant. The writer of Hebrews was doing his best help transition them out of that old system and fully into the message of grace and truth through Jesus. So, he uses the examples that they knew, Jewish history.

Moses led the people out of slavery, but that entire generation died in the wilderness (except Joshua and Caleb). The Promised Land was the land of rest for the Hebrews, but only a few folks ended up going to that land of rest. The reason they didn't make it wasn't because they didn't work hard enough, pray hard enough, or give enough. None of that mattered.

The reason they missed out on the rest God promised them was because they simply didn't believe God (Numbers 13-14). Believing God has to do with letting go and trusting Him. Simple as that. You don't have to work up belief. Just simple trust will do.

But in order trust Him, you must lose trust in yourself and let go of your own abilities to achieve goodness and perfection. The Israelites weren't willing to retire from their efforts and to trust in God's promises, so they didn't enter the rest. Literally, for them that meant wandering around the wilderness until they died. Kind of sucks, right?

The writer of Hebrews is warning the Hebrews of the 1st century who witnessed the death and resurrection of Christ of the same fate. Death, not in an actual wilderness, but in a spiritual one wandering around for years trying to re-accomplish what Christ had already accomplished, still trying to make sacrifices on behalf of their sins. But Christ had already come, and His sacrifice was their complete redemption.

Put Down Your Cross and Take Up His Life

Jesus didn't want us to find our own crosses to carry. You see, we must ask the important questions: if Jesus was asking us to follow Him, then where was He going? Once He picked up His cross and went somewhere... where on earth could He have been headed?

Well, to Calvary of course – to die. And that happened once, and only once. (*See* Romans 6:9-10). When He carried His cross up to Golgotha, we were in Him. When His hands were nailed, our hands were nailed. When He died, we died. When He was raised, we were raised. (*See* Galatians 2:20 and Colossians 3:3). We don't get our own death. He did what we couldn't do. Romans 6:10-11, (NIV) reads, *"The death he died, he died to sin once for all; but the life he lives, he lives to God. In the same way, count yourselves dead to sin but alive to God in Christ Jesus."* If someone wants to live a crucified life, then I'd challenge them to consider themselves already dead and raised from the grave.

Some have said, "Don't try to come down from your personal cross. You have to live a life that recognizes our continual crucifixion, constantly dying to self, etc. etc." The truth is, Jesus is no longer on the cross. And neither are you. He is fully alive and so are you. Religion takes the words of God that are meant to bring life, peace, and joy and turns them into demands that bring death, depression, and destruction.

I have watched young and old use these words of Jesus as a means to push their agendas, getting believers to lay down their own dreams and join someone else's ministry cause. But I want to encourage you to see this call to take up your cross as good news and not a daily drudge.

Paul's Daily Death

There is another problem passage that people always bring up when we start talking about enjoying the life God has given you. "But Great, the Bible says that we have to die daily. How do you fit that into your joyful-living, co-crucified life revelation, eh?"

Remember, folks, context is always key. You can't pull one verse out of the Bible and make an anti-gospel theology out of it. Well, I guess you can, but I wouldn't advise it. In Bible interpretation, one of the major challenges I have seen with Christians and unbelievers is that they pick up one passage in the Bible and run with it without caring what Jesus Christ had to say around that verse. This has given birth to false teachings, and once a Bible verse is given a wrong interpretation, it loses its relevance. The Bible is a coded book and until it is revealed to you by the Holy Spirit, you will make the Bible say what it's not saying.

Let's look at the actual verse in context. Paul is speaking to the Corinthian church and reminding them that he has gone to hell and back to preach the gospel of Jesus Christ. There were some in Corinth who were trying to convince them that there was no resurrection of the dead. Paul says to them: *"Why* [if there is no resurrection of the dead] *are we also in danger every hour? I affirm, brethren, by the boasting in you which I have in Christ Jesus our Lord, I die daily." 1Corinthians 15:30-31 (NASB)*

Paul tells these guys to stop worrying about Old Covenant rules and regulations about dietary laws, festivals dates, and holy days. He goes on to say that these things (old covenant laws and regulations) were shadows of the things that were to come. The writer of Hebrews expresses this same idea: *"For the Law, since it has only a shadow of the good things to come and not the very form of things."* *(Hebrews 10:1, NASB).*

What do you think of when you see a shadow of a person going by you? "I wonder who that is? I wonder how close they are?" We don't observe the shadow to figure out who the person is. We see the shadow and look up to see the person! Anytime you see a shadow, you start looking for its source. The shadow itself has no substance, but it serves to lead you to the object of its origin – the thing that carries reality. You embrace the person, not their shadow.

The entire Old Covenant is to be seen exactly that way. The prophets of the Old Covenant had revelation by the spirit of God of things to come and of God's will concerning certain events and people, but they didn't have complete understanding of Him. They experienced the character and nature of God but only as a shadow.

It was not until Christ came that the substance of that shadow appeared in full view. When He came, there was no need to go further into the shadows unless it was to remind us why the substance is really in front of us and maybe to laugh at our earlier conclusions of what we thought the substance might actually look like.

So, what does this mean for us today? And why are we talking about it? We must remember: if there is an Old Covenant passage saying something about God we don't see to be true in the person of Jesus Christ, then we have to re-approach that verse through the lens of Jesus Christ.

Don't cough up your decaf too quickly. I didn't say the passage isn't true or that it's wrong; I simply said that we must re-approach our conclusions about what that passage is trying to communicate considering our current conclusion about Christ.

The covenant given by Moses carried with it signs, wonders, and miracles. The parting of the Red Sea, the plagues of Egypt, the manna from heaven, and all the other supernatural activities involved were small considering what has been given to us in Christ Jesus.

Even Moses and his glow-worm trick couldn't outdo the strobe light of what we have in the New Covenant. Literally, Paul said that the Old Covenant, in comparison to the New, had no glory. Take it from Paul himself. He experienced both, and he was an expert in the Old.

After seeing the mystery revealed, he had nothing more to say about the mysterious shadow except that it was a shadow and had no substance in and of itself. This approach to the Old Covenant will be extremely helpful when we come across verses that seem to contradict what we know to be true about Jesus Christ.

Back to our original topic... When the Bible says that sin separates us from God, we must look at it considering the person and work of Christ and considering what we know to be true about the New Covenant. Let's look at this: Isaiah 59:2 (NASB) reads, *"But your iniquities have made a separation between you and your God, And your sins have hidden His face from you so that He does not hear."*

Do our sins really sever us from God? Do our sins cause God to be far from us and unable to hear our prayers? What does the New Convent have to say about this situation?

Colossians 1:21-22a, (NASB) reads, *"And although you were formerly alienated and hostile in mind, engaged in evil deeds, yet He has now reconciled you in His fleshly body thought death".*

The word "alienated" in the original language means "to be shut out from one's fellowship and intimacy." God didn't shut us out from fellowship with Him. We shut ourselves out. Sure, He closed the doors of Eden, but fellowship wasn't found in Eden. Fellowship was found in our hearts. That's why we still see men like Enoch and Abraham continuing to find fellowship with God after the fall.

Adam's sin didn't alienate God from Adam; it alienated Adam from God. Paul says in Colossians 1:21 that we became enemies of God in our minds. God was never our enemy, but we sure thought He was. When Adam and Eve sinned, instead of running to God, they ran and tried to hide from God. Why? Because they felt ashamed and had no idea what His reaction might be. They immediately became "enemies in their minds engaged in evil deeds."

The lie we believe that causes us to engage in sin is the same lie perpetuated after we engage in that behavior: "God is not a good Father and hasn't provided what you need. He's not really fully on your side. You should go ahead and lie, cheat, steal, fornicate, etc. to fulfill that need."

Once you go through with the action, there is nothing left to do but go deeper into hiding from God, because if He wasn't mad at you before, then He's mad at you now. If He wasn't your enemy before, then He is now.

This is the kind of thinking that keeps people living in their sin cycles. All the while, God is for us, loves us, and longs for us to come out from our hiding and embrace His forgiveness that has been available the whole time. Does sin separate us from God? Does it cause Him to turn His back in distain? Does it make Him run for fear of getting stained by our mistakes? I would like you to look at yourself in the mirror and give an emphatic "Hell no!"

Considering the reality of God expressed in and through Christ, we see that sin didn't actually separate us from God. But it changed our mindset about God, not that we should *"sin so that grace might abound,"* but the revelation of His nearness is what brings life transformation! (*See* Romans 6:1-2).

God wants us to come to Him when we struggle or fail. He is completely unmoved and unhindered by our sin. In fact, He doesn't relate to us based upon our sin any longer. He relates to us based upon His gift of righteousness. Jesus Christ completely became our sin when He was on the cross. When He became our sin, He was no less God than God the Father was. God never abandoned Jesus because God cannot abandon Himself. You are just as righteous as Jesus, and God will never abandon you.

Our Restored Position

In Adam, humanity lost its position as rulers of the earth and came under the dominion of darkness. But in Christ, we have been fully redeemed and restored to our original position. Ephesians 2:4-7 (NASB) declares, *"But God, being rich in mercy, because of His great love with which He loved us, even when we were dead in our transgressions, made us alive together with Christ (by grace you have been saved), and raised us up with Him, and seated us with him in the heavenly places in Christ Jesus, so that in the ages to come He might show the surpassing riches of His grace in kindness toward us in Christ Jesus."*

When Christ died and rose from the dead, He took us with Him. Jesus Christ is forever the vicarious man (the substitute) for all Mankind. With all the talk about the elect and the chosen, we often forget to talk about the One who we know is chosen and elect: Jesus Christ. He is the One Man who did what no man could do. He kept our side of the bargain in relationship with the Father and put us back in good standing with God. Adam dropped us low, but Jesus brought us high.

The Day God Threw a Keg-Party

I promise, God doesn't want to kill you! As I've looked back at the main teachings in the evangelical church, I can't help but feel like God is being presented as a bit schizophrenic.

The contradictions between the God who is angry at people and the God who loves people was hard to come to terms with. Reconciling the God who loves me and the God who may or may not be causing damage to my life was interesting, to say the least.

As a young believer I didn't know what else to do with the contradictions, so I just believed them and went on trusting God. At times, it seems that the God who is preached from some of the pulpits of the world is more like Zeus, or even Satan himself, than Jesus Christ.

"God's gonna send another tornado because the gays are destroying America."

"God's sending an earthquake to California because of abortion."

"God destroying your city because of the witchcraft happening there."

"America is under God's judgment because of Hollywood's influence on the world."

I understand there are many Old Testament stories that have to do with God sending judgment on a nation or city. But I also know we have a new lens with which to see God that the writers of the Old Testament did not have.

Before you throw stones, check out Hebrews 1:1-3a *(NASB): "God, after He spoke long ago to the fathers in the prophets in many portions and in many ways, in these last days has spoken to us in His Son, whom He appointed heir of all things, through whom also He made the world. And He is the radiance of His glory and the exact representation of His nature, and upholds all things by the word of His power..."*

Did I read this correctly? Did he just say that God used to speak through the prophets, but now He has spoken through Jesus? What does that mean? Over the past 6 years I have had my times of wanting to be like the Old Testament prophets. I mean, who wouldn't, right? These guys seemed like they knew God so well, and God trusted them with what He wanted to say to people on the earth.

But as I began reading verses like the ones in Hebrews, I began to rethink the desire to be a part of the Enoch company or the Elijah generation. If God spoke "long age" through the prophets "but now" He has spoken to us through Jesus, then I might want to pay more attention to Jesus than I do the prophets. I know God spoke through the prophets, but it seems like He did something through Jesus Christ that is much more deserving of our attention. The prophets talked about God. Jesus knew God. Oh, and don't forget the fact that He is God.

Look at this conversation that Jesus had with Phillip: *"Philip said to Him, 'Lord, show us the Father, and it is enough for us.' Jesus said to him, 'Have I been so long with you, and yet you have not come to know Me, Philip? He who has seen Me has seen the Father; how can you say, 'Show us the father'?"* (John 14:8-9, NASB).

If you've been in Church for more than a few weeks, then you've probably heard this Scripture. But in order to feel the real implications of what Jesus said here, we've got to go back and look at the context. What was Jesus saying and how did it impact His original audience? These were good Jewish boys who had grown up expecting the Messiah to come and deliver the Jews from Roman rule.

They knew the Messiah would be raised up by God, and many even believed he would come directly from heaven. (*See* Daniel 7). But they didn't have much of a grid for this Messiah being equal to God and weren't expecting Him to come saying that He is God.

This had to freak them out...at least a little? Jesus looked at these good Jewish boys and said, "You guys have been waiting to see God, but guess what... here I Am! He is Me and I am Him, we are one and have always been one from the beginning. If you've seen Me, then you have sent Him."

Look at this one from the Apostle John: *"No one has ever seen God, but the one and only Son, who is himself God and is in closest relationship with the Father, has made him known."* (John 1:18, NIV).

No one has ever seen God? Ummm... John, are you sure about that? I mean, seriously tons of folks have seen God.

So, I guess those guys who lived in the time of the law and the prophets who thought they had seen and known Him didn't see or know Him. Sure, they had a glimpse. But it was just that... A glimpse.

Look at the time before Jesus came...

Moses saw God on the mountain. Abraham spoke to God like a friend speaks to a friend: face to face. Enoch walked with God (so I assume that he saw Him). I could go on. "No," says John, "No one has seen Him. Jesus is the only one who truly knows Him because He is Him."

Jesus came and showed us something that was not just a glimpse but a perfectly clear representation. Jesus Himself has more to say about this.

"And the Father who sent Me, He has testified of Me. You have neither heard His voice at any time nor seen His form." (John 5:37, NASB).

Again, we must look at the context. Jesus is speaking to good Jewish folk who have heard God's voice through the prophets of old. Now, could this Jesus guy come along telling me that I have never heard God's voice before? This would be more than disconcerting to me, and devastating. It's no wonder these guys wanted to crucify Him. He basically came along discrediting everything they thought they knew about God, and then said He Himself was God.

If we are going to study the Bible, which I highly recommend, then we should probably do so in context of the person of Jesus and not through the darkened lenses of Old Covenant prophets who have never seen or known God.

If Jesus is God, then we have a massive problem. It might mean that some of our theological conclusions were not just a little off but altogether stupid. At least, that's what those good Jewish boys and girls realized when they came face to face with the One they supposedly knew everything about. Or would we be a little put off by some of His non-Christian habits and non-Christian friends?

No Mixture of Grace with The Law

You can't mix grace and law. You can't mix the old system and the new. You can't put old wine in a new wineskin. You can't hold onto shadow when the substance is standing right in front of you! It's just total nonsense and foolishness.

The Cross forgave Man's sins -
Past, Present, and Future. Complete package.

The danger of the early Hebrew church was that they continued to embrace grace and law – the old and the new – their works and His work. Paul stated it early to the Galatians who wanted to keep working for their salvation and sanctification: *"For through the law I died to the law so that I might live to God. I have been crucified with Christ and I no longer live, but Christ lives in me. The life I now live in the body, I live by faith in the Son of God, who loved me and gave himself for me. I do not set aside the grace of God, for if righteousness could be gained through the law, Christ died for nothing!"* Galatians 2:19-21 (NIV)

You don't have to add your part to the mix. Trusting in our own work is like taking the grace of God and strapping it in the backseat while you take the wheel of your own spirituality. My advice to you is this: go ahead and take the backseat. Hand over the wheel to Jesus and let His grace take you on the journey of being holy and joyful, living apart from your own works.

Stop trying to help grace save you. Stop trying to ask for forgiveness from God every second and minute. Confess Jesus as your Lord and Savior, and you are saved once and for all. All your sins past, present, and future are forgiven. Beloved, it's as simple as that. The Scriptures declared this boldly. It's not my own words.

Okay, look at Acts 13:38-39: *"Therefore, my friends, I want you to know that through Jesus the forgiveness of sins is proclaimed to you. Through him everyone who believes is set free from every sin, a justification you were not able to obtain under the law of Moses."* (NIV). This is the unadulterated, simple truth of the gospel.

If the content of this book makes you frustrated or angry, that's okay! It made me angry as well, as early as 2012 when I started getting a better knowledge and revelation of the finished works of Jesus from the Bible.

I was a pretty zealous religionist in the past. Fasting weekly, praying 9 hours per day, reading my Bible religiously, and condemning myself if I didn't talk to people about Jesus almost everywhere, I went. Those are just a few things that defined my life before I was touched by the revelation of grace. Letting go of religious efforts was like someone stripping drugs from an addict. I soon began to realize that I had been the master of my own spirituality.

You might be in the same boat as I was – trusting in your spiritual disciplines and effort to keep you strong in the faith. Here are some good questions to ask yourself:

On the days that you don't get to spend time in focused prayer and Bible reading, do you feel further from God or less spiritual than on days that you do those things?

If you stumble in any kind of sin, do you feel less spiritual or like you can't approach God confidently and with joy?

Do you always feel like you could be or should be doing more for God?

Do you live with a sense that God is disappointed in you?

Do you live with a sense of peace, joy, and contentment regardless of your performance?

If you answer yes to questions 1-4 and no to question 5, then I have good news for you! You are up for retirement. That's right. Retire. Rest. Take a good ole' nap in the glorious gospel. Retire, and live on full kingdom benefits that Jesus Christ has purchased for you through his blood.

Retire, beloved. Jesus did the job that you couldn't do, and He is faithful to keep you. You didn't save yourself, and you can't keep yourself saved. You are a son and not a slave. You don't owe God anything, absolutely nothing. You never did. He was never banking on you to make up for your failures and faults. He took care of those long before you ever realized it.

You are perfectly clean, perfectly loved, and perfectly forgiven. In the eyes of God, you are as holy as He is. Why? Because you are hidden in Christ Jesus. (*See* Colossians 3:3).

Today, retire from your works and enter the rest of the gospel and ultimately...perfection. If you've spent more than a couple Sundays in church, then you have probably heard something like this:

- "None of us is perfect. We are all on the journey."

- "Only God is Holy, we are just sinners saved by grace."

- "Someday, when we die, we will be perfect in the sweet by and by."

- "Well, don't get too cocky, young man. You'll never be perfect or holy until you get to heaven."

Really? Death is my guarantee of holiness? Death is my sure sanctification? So, you are telling me that I have been "saved" into a religious system that keeps me feeling bad for every bad thing I do, but I am destined to continue doing those bad things until I die? That's rather unfortunate news, and it's not a club I'd want to join.

But the good news is that every believer is perfect. Perfection is not a terminus. Perfection is a person and that person, is Jesus Christ. He is our perfection. So, when next you hear someone say that you are not perfect, tell such a one that you are perfect. It's not by your own doing. It's Jesus death that gave you that status.

What have we been saved from and what have we been saved into? Most Christians will tell you we have been saved from hell and saved into heaven. But could it be bigger than that? And possibly better than that? Yes! The death of Jesus on the cross was not just about saving Mankind from Hell fire. It's far bigger than that. It's about perfection, righteousness, and relationship with God the Father. Even when you fall into sin, any kind of sin, confess your righteousness in Him boldly. Walk out in confidence and joy. Throw away that guilt that tries to take hold of your mind. Remind yourself of your righteous position in Christ.

The legalistic Christians will say this is encouraging people to sin. Well, I'd like you to know that as long as we are under this flesh, we will continue to make mistakes. At different periods in our new creation life, we will all experience, thousands of times, circumstances where our flesh will tend to weaken us.

We are humans. Nobody is perfect or above sin, no matter how highly spiritual he or she may be. The Pope, the Bishops, the Archbishops, Pastors, Apostles, Prophets, Evangelists and even you and me. No one is sinless in this life.

In churches today and around our religious communities, many Christians have a habit of classifying sins as big or small in order to make themselves look more holy or better than another person. This is totally wrong. In the eyes of God, all sins are sins. The person who cheats people through internet fraud and scams is no different from that person who is guilty of murder.

The person who envies his neighbor is no different from a person who commits fornication or adultery. The pastor who steals from his church finances is not different from that prostitute on the street. In the eyes of God, they are all sinners.

There is no such thing as small or big sin. Sin is sin. But the good news is that Jesus has paid the wages of sin on our behalf. God has forgiven us all our past, present, and future sins. What a complete package. This is the beauty of grace, and only the blood of Jesus Christ could accomplish this.

*Let your life be a visible display
of God's invisible kingdom.*

Now, the question is: does this mean that because you are saved or because all your sins are forgiven that you should live life any way or toss away morality and good character? Of course, that is a No. In as much as morality doesn't take you to heaven or earn you any spiritual reward or blessings, morality is expected from us all as ambassadors of Christ Jesus.

In as much as God doesn't judge you by your demeanor or character, the world for sure will continue to judge you by your conduct and character every day. So, our life on earth should model that of Jesus Christ. Jesus was a peaceful person who lived in unity among those in His community. Jesus was not a murderer, a thief, or a dishonest person. Jesus was not egotistical., He showed empathy and kindness to everyone irrespective of race, religion, or financial background.

This is the kind of conduct expected of us as Jesus' followers. You cannot be mean and disrespectful to people and expect them to see Jesus in you. Our lifestyle, our actions are the easier channel to validate or showcase the presence of Jesus in our lives. Folks in our communities don't see Jesus Christ or God, but they can see Him through our actions and conduct.

One of my prayers every day is that God will continue to help me live a life that will be a visible display of His invisible kingdom. This day, people are not interested in your words, they are interested in your actions.

When I was a teen, my mum always reminded me to show people Jesus through my actions and not my words. I have grown up believing this statement from my sweet mother to be true.

CHAPTER 11

THE MISREPRESENTED GOD

Religion has told so many lies about the nature and personality of God. I have in times past believed such lies. Lies that tend to depict God as a very wicked Father or one who derives joy from seeing His children suffer. Then I found the truth.

Many of the traits we have attributed to God are not only false but are the very traits of Satan himself. Religion has created a false god, one of true horror, and shoved this concept so deeply down our throats that to even question it is often labeled blasphemy.

Lies like you must give God your tithe before He can bless you. God hates sinners. God chooses or shows you your wife or husband to be. God is angry at the world. God sends temptations to His children or sends affliction on them just so they can listen to Him or change their ways.

If you have ever looked at a couple of hormonal teenagers and thought to yourself, "Those kids don't know the first thing about love," then you may have a fair idea of how God thinks about some of us. We hardly know the first thing about love. You only must listen to the way we talk to others to know that this is fact.

We tell others that we want to be "Used by God" as if love ever uses people. We boast of our "commitment to Christ" as if the substance of love consists of making promises. We testify that God has sent us into the wilderness or made us sick to teach us things, as if God would ever do such things. And then we wonder why the folks listening don't want to know Him!!! Whatever we believe about love, we believe about God; for God is love personified. Friend, this is a profound truth. God is love.

If your definition of love has been filtered through our fallenness and twisted by religion, you will inevitably end up with a screwy picture of God. This is the chief reason why so many people who claim to know God are miserable. They have been told that God values us as servants and that He relates to us as a general relates to a soldier. "Relationship" for them is not about enjoying life together but following orders. It's a monologue rather than a dialogue.

Your love for people is the evidence of God's presence in you.

Unfortunately, a mixed-up view of God's love has a devastating effect our relationships with others. For instance, there are those who worry that they may be loving their spouses or their children too much. They fear they may be turning their loved ones into idols and incurring the jealousy of a vengeful God.

I'm always bewildered when I hear people boastfully say, "I love God more than my wife." The only way to love God more than your spouse is to love God through your spouse. Your husband or wife would be the direct recipient of the love. The God, who is love, loves it when we love.

God is never in competition with your love for people! Any time you love a person, you are not far from God, you are depicting His personality. Then there are those who love their family too little, possibly because they believe that family distracts them from some higher calling, such as ministry. Nothing could be further from the truth.

Your love for people is the evidence that God is living inside you. It surprises me to see so many people who honestly believe that God desires a separate and secret relationship with them aside from their family members.

Many men will lock themselves in their prayer closets while their wives are in another room watching the kids alone. Religion has sold us a bunch of lies about the love of God. We have been told that God is envious, distrustful, needy, angry, distant, and that He keeps a record of wrongs.

Fall for these lies and it will de-humanize you. You'll waste your life trying to force-fit your dreams and desires into a religious fungus, and you'll be utterly miserable. If you're already miserable or you just want a clearer picture of what God is really like, then am glad you picked this book. I also recommend that you get a copy of my next book, *The Misrepresented God.* That's where you will get a full *Epignosis* of the true nature and personality of God, backed up with relevant Scriptural references.

God never envies anyone or anything. He never desires to take for Himself what others have. Instead, He longs to give away all He has... He keeps no record of the wrong things you've done because He refuses to call you by the name of your past... God is perseverance personified, proving He is who He claims to be. He stands in the storm and walks through the fire simply to express His love for you. He will never fail you, never fall short, never fall out of love, because He's made of love, the very source of it all. He is Creator of the beginning who has no beginning.

The Unprinted Rules of Love

Paul famously prayed that we would know the measureless love of God, for it's in knowing His love that we truly live. So how do we come to know His love? God's love is experienced in loving people. When you truly love someone unconditionally... that flame of love inside your heart is God.

Okay Great, how do I come to love someone unconditionally? Well friend, this kind of love comes as a result of knowing how much God loves you. When I came to the knowledge that God is crazy about me for no other reason than that I am his son, I began to love others even more. Selfishness died in me. I became more sacrificial and empathetic towards others.

The love of God is experienced through loving people, but the love for people only comes when you come to the awareness of the unconditional love of God for you. Jesus didn't come to recruit servants but to give us abundant life founded on the Father's unrestricted love.

The Lies that has been told about God

Have you heard a sermon like this? "If you think there's any good in you, you better hold on for your life because God's about to knock you off your throne and expose the truth of how wicked you really are." "Hallelujah!" The crowd urged the preacher on, showing their approval by raising their hands as if to say, "It's happened to me, and I liked it!" "He's not gonna share His glory with you or anyone else!" "Preach it!" came a voice from someone in the front row. "God is God, and the sooner you realize that the better of you'll be, and if He's got to take one of your children homes to get your attention, He'll do it!" "That's right – yes He will," came another voice, while a few others nodded their heads and clapped their hands.

The image of the old church that I grew up in has been indelibly etched into my mind. This new life and knowledge can be a little bit scary, but in an exciting sort of way. The God they told me about in my Sunday school classes in church was not someone I would want to be friends with. I remember thinking how unfortunate it was that we had to *love* Him in order to go to heaven.

Something must be clearly wrong with how we see our God if this is how most Christians think. So many people live in fear of Jesus Christ's return. What is supposed to be the most beautiful day of all to Christians has been used against us to the point where we now live in fear of its arrival.

However, your relationship with God is an adventure tailor-made by Him just for you. Paul said the love of Christ surpasses knowledge (Ephesians 3:19). His love is so great, it's not reducible to rules or books. It's easier to say what the love of God isn't like.

God is not proud, rude, or self-seeking. He is not provoked, and He thinks no evil of you. In short, God is nothing like the evil picture painted of Him by religion. But when it comes to discovering the fullness of what God is like, well that's the Great Adventure of Life!

I can sit through two hours of Christin television and watched six sermons in a row. Each sermon directly contradicts the others, and no one even questions it. A pastor will come to our church and preach a sermon on how God will never leave us or forsake us, and sixty seconds later he follows up with an insinuation that He just might. We listen to teachings of God's promises and how they are a gift, followed by a list of things we must do in order to earn them.

There are between thirty and forty thousand different Christian denominations, each contradicting the other in some way. Logic alone would dictate that it is next to impossible to know God by way of church teachings. Our religion today, with its promises and testimonies reminds me of a group of grandmothers exchanging their old wives' tales and swearing by them to their dying day.

With each generation, the tale gets a little more overstated and exaggerated, until finally we are left with a religion that bears no resemblance to the truth and teachings that tell about a God who never existed.

I am quickly coming to believe that this is the first time in history that people outside the church have shown more signs of knowing God's heart than the people within the church.

People in the world shake their heads in disgust at the things we teach about God because they just know it's erroneous, but for some reason most Christians don't see it. I have found that the common bar dweller knows more about the heart of God than the dedicated churchgoer. Many Christians think they know God because they read about him in a book.

We've been taught that the more we read the Bible, the more we will know Him. The Pharisees knew the Scripture like the back of their hands, but when God stood right in front of them, they just refused to believe He was the One they read about.

Relationship with God to this generation of Christianity is only about reading the Bible. In fact, we believe this so much that we have even exchanged God for the Bible, attributing all the attributes of God Himself to it. If we don't read it excessively or understand it, we feel lost and unspiritual. We feel a million miles from God. But God is more than our Bible, He is bigger than our bible. The bible is too small to fully speak of the Sovereignty and "Deitism" of God.

I once heard that the definition of insanity is when a person does the same thing over and over expecting different results. I have often wondered if religion has the power to take people's sanity. We are constantly taught to deny the truth about the results and believe that something else will take place the next time around.

The things we put our faith in and preach to the world are clearly not working, yet we continue to act and talk as if they are. We tithe 10 percent of our incomes and when the recession comes, we see just as many religious people go bankrupt as people who are unreligious.

We say, "a family that prays together stays together." Yet research done by www.religioustolerance.com indicates that the divorce rate is actually higher in the church than it is outside the church. We claim to have power and peace and joy and spiritual understanding, but in the end, it seems a similar number of people in the church are on medication for depression, anxiety, ADHD, and a host of other emotional problems.

I believe the heart of God is broken over His children's lack of knowledge of who He is. Not livid or vengeful, but simply broken. Imagine having the very one who was supposed to know you better than anyone in the world not even know your name. That is precisely how God feels with this generation.

Jesus Christ is the express image of God.

My desire is to bring not condemnation but freedom to the body of Christ. I do not believe that the answer is to pray for power or fire from heaven to make it all go away. The answer is quite simple. We need truth. We need to come to the true knowledge of the nature of God and how much He loves mankind. Thank God for all the wonderful teachers of the gospel out there who are assiduously revealing the truth of the nature and personality of God through Jesus Christ.

I refuse to believe in the Personality many preachers and prophets old or new, portrayed God to be. I refuse to even believe how certain Old Testament Scriptures portrayed God. I choose to believe the God who manifested Himself in the person of Jesus Christ who loves mankind more than we love ourselves. That is the God I know.

I choose to believe in the God who fed the poor and healed the sick without asking for a requirement to be met. The God who loved the sinners and dined with the tax collectors, the thieves, and the prostitutes. The God who never discriminated, killed, or got angry at anyone. The God who gave His life for mankind.

When it comes to experiencing the love of God, I don't have all the answers – I don't even have all the questions! But I know I would rather be lost in His arms of love than found in the shackles of the loveless law.

Have you ever listened to a preacher talk about God and thought, "That doesn't sound like God"? Millions have become repulsed by the God some churches describes. From birth, many Christians have been bombarded with so many contradictory teachings and doctrines that their understanding of God bears a resemblance to a tightly tangled ball of Christmas tree lights.

With so many confusing teachings about God and countless contradictions, misunderstandings, outright scams, and simplistic fear-based teachings, how can we really know who God is? No educated theologians or credentialed pastors have a corner on the truth about God. He is not locked in a monastery high in the mountains. He's not sitting in church hoping you'll show up. He's not simply out traveling with the latest super-spiritual faith healer.

Beloved, Knowing God is easier than any of us imagines. People who have spent years searching for the truth about Him can finally discover that they have known Him all along. Knowing God is as easy as learning what love means. His character and personality can be known and understood.

If you know what love is or have experienced true and unconditional love, then you already know God. But His love is far purer and abounding than any love you will ever experience. I hear some folks say we know God by revelation. Friend, God is your Father and you need no revelation to know him. He has revealed Himself to you through Jesus Christ.

Many are pleading that God should not take the Holy Spirit from them. After the cross, the Holy Spirit dwells in the believer forever. No need for believers in Christ to be waiting for the Holy Spirit to come again, He has already come, and He will abide with the believer forever.

There are those who are trying to amplify the presence of God today by utilizing prayer shawls and shofars when Jesus moved us from worshipping or seeing him through places and objects 2000 years ago. You do not need anyone to take your prayer request to Jerusalem. There is nothing special about Jerusalem anymore for the believer. Jesus is everywhere.

People are trying to create Jesus of the Jews (Judaism). After the cross, he is Jesus of the Jews and Gentiles. The Jews and Gentiles are now collapsed in one new Man. Galatians 3:28 read, *"There is neither Jew nor Greek, there is neither bond nor free, there is neither male nor female: for ye are all one in Christ Jesus."*

Christians are still fighting the devil and the flesh as though Jesus did not do a complete work 2000 years ago. Paul wrote to the believers in Colossians reminding them about the finished work of Jesus saying; *"Blotting out the handwriting of ordinances that was against us, which was contrary to us, and took it out of the way, nailing it to his cross; And having spoiled principalities and powers, he made a shew of them openly, triumphing over them in it."* (Colossians 2:14-15).

The Fall Didn't Screw Up God's Plan

Somewhere along the way, we got this strange idea that when Adam sinned, the heavens were shut up, and God turned to cosmic bowling and stargazing. "Well, I guess I'll have to wait about 4,000 years until Jesus dies for them so I can be friends with them again." Folks, this was not the case.

Before we fell in Adam, we were found in Christ. God didn't see Adam's sin and say, "Oh crap. Well, back to the drawing board, boys." No, His plans were not disenchanted. Even though Adam's mind was tainted with sin and deception, God was still closer than the air Adam breathed, and Adam still bore God's image.

Look what God said after the fall and before the coming of Christ: *"for in the image of God has God made mankind."* (Genesis 9:6, NIV). The fall didn't change God's view of Man, but it changed Man's view of God – and of himself. God has no problem loving Mankind all the way through. He was obviously available to anyone at any time.

We find that before Moses brought the law, there were many people who found God, or rather, realized that He was never gone to begin with. There were other folks who seemed to realize God's love and kindness towards them before it had been clearly revealed in Christ. For example, Enoch walked with God in a pretty intimate way.

Abraham and Elijah did similarly. David is one of my favorites. After his six-month season of sin, he repented by saying, "God, I know you got me out of that sinful season and brought me back to you because you enjoy me so much." (*See* Psalms 18:19).

These men knew something about God that many people had lost. Each one of them seemed to pass through the veil of Old Covenant thinking and find that, all along, their sin was not the main issue but rather, their view of God was. While many were still trying to appease God through rituals and rules, these guys realized that God already liked them and that He still wanted friendship with them. He was not their enemy. Through Christ, God has shown that mankind has always been in His heart.

There was never a time when God desired to be apart from Mankind. Becoming a man in Christ confirmed that Mankind's origin was not in the fall of Adam but in the position of Christ – at the right hand of God. Our fall was great, but His grace was greater.

Your identity is not in what you've done or what others say about you. Your identity is found in Christ and Christ alone – what He has done for you and what He has said about you.

His declaration about mankind from the beginning was "he is very good." (*See* Genesis 1:31). Our sin didn't reverse this declaration in God's mind. It was only in our minds. Our fall didn't cause God to back away from us; it only caused us to turn our backs on Him. Even still, He loves each one of us and desires that all men would come to the knowledge of the truth. (1 Timothy 2:4).

What truth? The truth of His love of us. Every person on the face of the planet was created by Him and for Him. God didn't create some for His pleasure and some for His displeasure. Instead, all men were created to bring Him joy and pleasure. God's will from the very beginning was to create for His enjoyment and for His pleasure. And of course, the crown of that creation was and still is His children – the ones who are made in His image, that is, all of humanity.

We all know we are made for relationship. That's why we like to be together during the most important times in life. One of the health challenges people all over the world faced during the Covid-19 (Coronavirus) pandemic was loneliness and depression. The lockdown was difficult for people because Mankind was created for relationship. We are social beings, and when you take that part of our life away, people can go wild and become dangerous to themselves and those around them. None of us enjoy being alone. There is a true sense of togetherness we all enjoy.

We were made for relationship. Together with God, together with one another. Found in Him. As a family. And this togetherness is the answer to life's deepest questions. Not that we come to perfect conclusions, but we go on the journey together. Maybe the entire point of existence is to be together, as one, with God and with one another – learning from one another about what is most important. God is a Family Man, who loves for His children of which you are one, to relate with him from a father figure perspective not like a faraway Deity.

CHAPTER 12

GRACE VERSUS THE LAW

The word grace goes far beyond being a mere cliché. Instead it describes the very character of God, telling of who God is. The word grace was translated from the Greek word *charis*, which means underserved favor, or unmerited favor.

The grace of God describes the character of God in that He gave up His Son to die. We see Paul teach the grace of God as salvation. Titus 2:11 reads, *"For the grace of God that bringeth salvation hath appeared to all men."* Ephesians 2:4-8 declares, *"But God, who is rich in mercy, for his great love wherewith he loved us, Even when we were dead in sins, hath quickened us together with Christ, (by grace ye are saved;) And hath raised us up together, and made us sit together in heavenly places in Christ Jesus: That in the ages to come he might shew the exceeding riches of his grace in his kindness toward us through Christ Jesus. For by grace are ye saved through faith; and that not of yourselves: It the gift of God."*

Paul also taught that all believers have received grace in Christ Jesus: saying; *"Being justified freely by his grace through the redemption that is in Christ Jesus: Whom God hath set forth to be a propitiation through faith in his blood, to declare his righteousness for the remission of sins that are past, through the forbearance of God." Romans 3:24-25.*

Ephesians 1:6-7 reads, *"To the praise of the glory of his grace, wherein he hath made us accepted in the beloved. In whom we have redemption through his blood, the forgiveness of sins, according to the riches of his grace."*

Everything we enjoy today as children of God is based on the grace of God. In the Old Testament, the basis for God's blessings was dependent on the law. After the cross, the basis for God's blessing is faith in the finished work of Christ. The law says you are accepted by God if you keep all the commandments and meets all its obligations. But grace says God has accepted you, not because you kept the standard, but because Jesus has kept the standard for you. (*See* Romans 4:13-16).

The moment you place the law of Moses between you and God, you are neglecting the finished work of Christ. It is an insult to the work of redemption. For if righteousness came through the law, then Christ died in vain. When the devil points to your feelings by the standard of the law, point him to the propitiation for your sins on the cross. Galatians 4:4-5 says, *"But when the fulness of the time was come, God sent forth his Son, made of a woman, made under the law, To redeem them that were under the law, that we might receive the adoption of sons."*

Christ has fulfilled the requirement of the law.

The law was Satan's greatest weapon against humanity, but Jesus has disarmed him by fulfilling all the demands of the law. The law always condemns and keeps men away from God. Some preachers preach law instead of grace. They say you are saved by grace but perfected by the law. We either live totally under grace or totally under the law. (*See* Romans 11:6).

The totality of the Christian life is purely lived from start to finish by grace. Romans 3:21-24 reads, *"But now the righteousness of God without the law is manifested, being witnessed by the law and the prophets; even the righteousness of God which is by faith of Jesus Christ unto all and upon all them that believe: for there is no difference: For all have sinned, and come short of the glory of God; Being justified freely by his grace through the redemption that is in Christ Jesus."*

The good news of the gospel is not in the death of Jesus Christ but rather in His Resurrection.

How did you receive Jesus Christ the Lord?

Ephesians 2:8 reads, *"For by grace are ye saved through faith; and that not of yourselves: it is the gift of God."* You received Him by grace through faith, so you walk in Him by grace through faith. Romans 8:3-4 reads, *"For what the law could not do, in that it was weak through the flesh, God sending his own Son in the likeness of sinful flesh, and for sin, condemned sin in the flesh: That the righteousness of the law might be fulfilled in us, who walk not after the flesh, but after the Spirit."*

Paul taught forgiveness of sins as the grace of God. So, the grace of God brings forgiveness of sins. (*See* Romans 3:24 & 5:1-2). He teaches righteousness as the grace of God. We can safely affirm that the grace of God is seen in all that Christ did for humanity, bringing justification, righteousness, forgiveness of sins, and therefore salvation to all men. All that Christ has done is embedded in the message of the gospel. This gospel is called the good news and here is that good news that saves: 1 Corinthians 15:1-4 reads, *"Moreover, brethren, I declare unto you the gospel which I preached unto you, which also ye have received, and wherein ye stand; but which also ye are saved, if ye keep in memory what I preached unto you, unless ye have believed in vain. For I delivered unto you first of all that which I also received, how that Christ died for our sins according to the scripture; and that he was buried, and that he rose again the third day according to the scriptures."*

The message of the gospel, as we saw in the earlier chapters, is the death, the burial, the resurrection, and the ascension of Jesus to the Father's right hand. Historical records can tell you that He died. The people who saw him die in Jerusalem, for example, knew He died for real. They didn't need faith to believe this fact.

There is therefore no faith involved in knowing Jesus died, neither is there faith involved in knowing that He was buried. That He rose from the dead is paramount. It is so crucial to comprehend that the message of the gospel after the cross is in the resurrection of Jesus. The good news of the gospel is not His death but in His resurrection. This must therefore be our focus in preaching.

For Us, As Us, In Us

God didn't leave us to our own devices and our own solutions. Instead, He made the decision for us and took care of the problem as us. In doing this, He showed us His continued and unbreakable commitment toward us. (*See* Romans 5:8). He laid down his life for those who didn't want anything to do with Him because He knew that we had forgotten who we were. We had given in to the false identity. That old Adamic self was full of deceit and destined to die, not as a punishment for sin but as the result of sin.

Christ came to reveal the Father, not to appease the Father. Christ came to express God's love for us. He came to show us God's love, not to make God love us. God never stopped loving us. He has always and will always love humanity. He is love embodied.

He decided, without a conference call with us, to take on the death that we inherited as a result of sin. He did not desire to continue His existence without us. He made us for Himself and planned an eternal friendship with us. He wouldn't have it any other way. So, what did He do? He died for us and Him as us. He tasted death and separation on behalf of us all. (*See* Hebrews 2:9, NASB).

God did not need a sacrifice, but we did. The cross didn't change God's mind about us. Rather it changed our minds about God. Jesus showed us that God was not angry with humanity, but humanity had become angry with God.

*Jesus Christ came to reveal the Father,
not to appease the Father.*

Not only did Jesus show us what God was like, but in His death, He transcendentally swallowed up the fallen and sinful self that Man had created through unbelief and rendered it powerless. Not only did He die for us, but He died as us. Just as Adam sinned as us (Romans 5:15-17), Jesus Christ did the same and decided to die as us (Romans 5:18).

In His death, He became us and destroyed the individual, separate, fallen identity that we had created through Adam. He became the false identity that we had taken on and completely obliterated it in His death in the cross. That is why Paul categorically says, "when one died all died." (2 Corinthians 5:14).

Therefore, today, I can emphatically declare that you are no longer a sinner if you believe in the finished works of Jesus for you. You no longer have a sinful nature, you are perfect.

You are holy.

You are complete.

You are justified.

And it's not your fault.

The cross didn't change God's mind about us
Rather it changed our minds about God.

Christ has swallowed you up in His life and death. Your life is now hidden with Christ inside of the ocean of God's love for all humanity. This is who you are. Jesus Christ's work was effective for you. "Well, Great, why do I still feel flawed?" Probably because you have yet to hear this good news. It's time to awaken to reality. See that you were in Him when He died. And consider yourself dead to sin.

You have been included in Christ's effective, completed work on the cross. You have been translated out of darkness, unbelief, depression, sickness, and sadness. All the effects of sin and the curse are no longer yours to embrace. That world is gone. Can you breathe air again? You are free to breathe the air of heaven. You are free to enjoy your everlasting life today.

When Jesus said, "It is finished", friend, He was not making a half-hearted declaration regarding His work on the cross. No! His plan was all-inclusive, and His work was fully finished. He left no part of your being out of the question in His death and resurrection. Sure, our experience tells us differently at times, but we don't live by our experiences. We live by faith in the Son of God.

You weren't partially crucified with Christ. You were fully included in His crucifixion. Your only job is to recognize this reality and set your mind on that truth. Apostle Paul recognized this and said, *"I have been crucified with Christ; and it is no longer I who live, but Christ lives in me; and the life which I now live in the flesh I live by the faith of the Son of God who loved me and gave Himself up for me."* (Galatians 2:20, NASB). Paul got it, He understood Christ's death was vicarious on our behalf, and our effort to include ourselves is not needed. Paul realized that within the body of Jesus was the entire human race and every bit of the false reality we had created through our rebellion.

Look what Paul said regarding our inclusion in Christ's death....

He said that when One died, all died. (2 Corinthians 5:14). Who was that One? Christ, of course. And who are the all? Everyone, of course. God didn't wait for you to be born in order to take care of your fallen nature. He didn't wait for you to get right with Him before He chose to forgive you in Christ.

As unfair as the sinful effect that came upon us all, so it is with the heavenly effect. Yet, Paul seemed to say that it was similar but not the same. In fact, he declares that the effect of Christ's work on the cross for all humanity was "much more" effective and far outweighed Adam's failure.

Check it out *Romans 5:15 (NASB)!! "But the free gift is not like the transgression. For if by the transgression of one the many died, much more did the grace of God and the gift by the grace of the one Man, Jesus Christ, abound to the many."*

Through Adam's sin, many died. Through Christ's death and resurrection, the many were influenced by grace. The judgment of guilt was passed on everyone because of what Adam did. But the free gift came to   declaring justification and right-standing before God. Adam's fall was swallowed up by Jesus' final act on the cross. So, what is there to do? Well, receive and rest in what He has done, and watch life.

Paul said, *"Or do you not know that all of us who have been baptized into Christ Jesus have been baptized into His death? Therefore, we have been with him through baptism into death, so that as Christ was raised from the dead through the glory of the Father, so we too might walk in newness of life."* (Romans 6:3-4, NASB).

Paul was not talking about your personal baptism in pastor Jim's swimming pool. I mean, sure He spoke in part of what you did when you were dunked or sprinkled in the holy chlorine water in your pastor's backyard or the muddy-holy water at your church's lake day. But that was only a representation of what took place 2,000 years ago when Christ baptized humanity into His death.

Jesus finished the job on the tree. In His one act He declared that you have been made righteous in Him. What Adam did, Jesus undid. What Adam tainted, Jesus sainted. He became our sin, and we became His rightness. He became our darkness, and we became His light. He became our failure and we became His success.

Your identity is completely found in Him and as Him. You don't get your own separate cross; you were united with Him on His cross. You were baptized into His death and raised to newness. Your prayer didn't save you. Christ saved you. When He died, you died. When He raised, you were raised. He only gets one death and you only get one death. In the same way that He died once to sin, you did too.

His death was yours, and that's a fact. He died for us and as us. He didn't wait for our permission to die our death, and He didn't wait for our consent to include us in His life. He chose, and He acted. Romans 6:10-11, NASB reads, *"For the death that He died, He died to sin once for all; but the life that He lives, He lives to God. Even so consider yourselves to be dead to sin, but alive to God in Christ Jesus.*

Your sinful nature was completely taken care of 2,000 years ago when Christ died. Just as circumcision could not be done by the child himself but had to be done by another, so Christ is the One who has circumcised our heart and removed the dirty old sinful nature without any assistance from us. This is great news!

You are no longer a sinner. You were included in the death, burial, and resurrection of Christ through His faithfulness. His pain was your gain, His death was your death, and His life is now your life.

Think about your worst failure, your greatest regret, your haunting memories.... Each one of those were dealt with on the cross of Christ, and they no longer define you at all. Those mistakes are no longer yours. They were actions done by a person who had forgotten his or her original design but who has now been awakened to the truth of inclusion in grace. Today, count yourself as being completely dead to the old you. Have a little funeral for it if need be, but don't live another day in relation to it.

Count yourself as being one who was dead and is now alive, wakened from the deathly sleep of unbelief. See yourself as perfect, holy, and beautiful. Look in the mirror and see the beauty of God shinning back at you. You are loved. You are holy. You are perfect. You are accepted.

CHAPTER 13

DEMYSTIFYING THE SUBJECT OF TITHING AND FASTING

Demystifying Tithing through the Lens of Grace:

One of the major avenues for fraud in Christendom, especially in Africa, is this thing called "tithing." All through my young Christian life I have not seen any Scriptures of the Old Testament so wrongly used against believers like this practice.

I grew up in one of the developing sub-Sahara nations where I saw with my own eyes how certain men and women used one verse of the Bible to defraud millions of saints. These clergymen are worth millions and millions of dollars; some have a private jet, while others have two to three jets, each worth millions of dollar.

People have complained that some pastors of today are materialistic. Yes, there are many pastors who are money-oriented, but there are genuinely men and women of God who are genuinely concerned about the body of Christ.

The subject of tithing has recently raised a series of questions and arguments in the body of Christ. Therefore, I have a burden in my heart to share with you from the Scriptures the truth about this subject. The truth backed up with facts from the Old Testament, the Gospels, and the Epistles, which is the climax of all revelations.

Many will hate me for writing this to you. I will be called all sort of names, but I refuse to endure watching this deception go on. Saints, it is time we grow up and start desiring the revelation of the Scriptures, because if we don't, men will continue to take advantage of our ignorance of the Word of God.

Now, I'd like you to know that I have been a faithful tither myself. In fact, I doubt if there was any more faithful in tithing than I was. I was faithful to the point of paying double whenever I missed paying my tithe. I paid tithe from my school fees back in college, paid tithe from every bit of money that came into my hands. Until I encountered revelation through the Scriptures, I was against anyone who rebelled against paying his or her tithe.

I have served in churches where tithing was used to measure one's commitment to the church. I have enforced the payment of tithing, and as a pastor, I had severally taught wrongly on the subject of tithing, cursing and raining condemnation on those who refused to pay or had financial impediments and were unable to pay their tithes to my church.

In some of the churches I served in, the consistent payment of tithe was a key requirement before any member could be given any leadership position in the church or receive any financial help from the church.

Thank God for revelation knowledge of His word. I'm free from being a victim of such fraud. And I hope through this book, you will receive the knowledge you need to break out of this bondage and become the better and cheerful giver that God expects you to be. Now, let's begin!!!

To understand the subject of tithing, we must look at it from a complete context of the Bible, the origin of it, who paid tithe first and who asked the first tither in the Bible to pay tithe. We must also consider the reason why tithing was introduced, and the audience being addressed in the Scripture.

We must also consider every Scripture of the Old Testament where "tithing" or "tithes" was mentioned, consider what the New Testament said about tithing (the Gospels, the Epistles), and most importantly, summarize our findings through the lens of Jesus Christ, whom we have seen from the previous chapter is the central message of the Bible and the express revelation of God the Father to Mankind.

I John 5:20 reads, *"And we know that the Son of God has come and has given us an understanding, that we may know Him who is true; and we are in Him who is true, in His Son Jesus Christ. This is the true God and eternal life."*

Our understanding is in the light of Christ. Jesus came to reveal the Father to humanity. Jesus Christ is the express revelation of God. (*See* Colossians 1:15; 26-29). So, through

Jesus the mystery of the Scriptures (Old Testament) and many of its texts, is revealed to Mankind.

The mystery of the Scriptures is God in Man. That God would make His abode in Man as we witness today was the mystery of the Old Testament. Christ in me, the hope of Glory. When we talk of the Scriptures, we are referring to the Old Testament. (*See* 2 Peter 1:20-21). The Scripture is also known as the Old Testament, the Torah, the mystery, or Jesus concealed.

When you read the Scriptures, you must subject them to the interpretation of the Epistles. Why? Because the Scriptures were written by men who never saw God, hence in their interpretation of God or what He says will be certain attributes wrongly attributed to the nature and character of God. Jesus said thus clearly in John 1:18.

Jesus is the only custodian of God and the only One who can reveal God to any man. Therefore, to know God, one must know Jesus. (John 14:7-8). Whatever Jesus does is what the Father does, and whatever Jesus did not do, the Father will not do and has never done. How do I know this? Because Jesus Christ said so. Jesus and God the Father are one.

Therefore, whatever the prophets, Moses, Malachi, Elijah, Ezekiel, Isaiah, etc., all said about God, must be subject to the character and personality of Jesus Christ. Jesus never killed, so God doesn't kill. Jesus healed all who were oppressed and sick, then God heals all. Jesus never discriminated, God doesn't. Jesus did not condemn or judge anyone, God doesn't. Jesus welcomed and loved the sinners; God also loves the sinners.

———————— ∿༄ ༄∿ ————————

To know God, one must see and know
Jesus Christ, for He is the express
image and revelation of God.

———————— ∿༄ ༄∿ ————————

Like I said earlier, I must give you a doctrinal, sound teaching on this issue of tithing, whether a new covenant/grace Christian should tithe or not tithe, because this topic is causing confusion in the body of Christ. I'd like you to understand that the Scriptures, Gospels, and Epistles are not loud on the topic of tithing.

Doctrinally, we should be loud on issues the Bible is loud on and silent on issues the Bible is silent on. The scripture will never mean today what it never meant when it was first spoken. God doesn't change. So, we must subject the subject of tithing, through the lens of Jesus Christ. (*See* Romans 16:25).

The New Testament is the revelation of the Old Testament (Scriptures). Also, the Bible says no Scripture is of any private interpretation. (*See* 2 Peter 1:20). We must stop interpreting the Bible to support our actions. Stop trying to make a private interpretation of the Scriptures. Allow the Scriptures to speak to you; stop trying to speak to them. It's wrong to use one passage, line, or verse of the Scriptures and turn it into a law or doctrine.

The Scriptures are absolute. We are not. So, stop trying to talk to the infallible and absolute Word of God. Allow it talk to you. The Scripture is *the* prophecy. What is the prophecy? The message. Who is the message? The man. Who is the man? Jesus Christ.

The prophecy (Jesus Christ) is the lens to use to judge all prophecies. Just because your pastor or prophet is preaching fire or prophesying rain and thunder, doesn't mean it's absolute. You must subject those prophecies to *the* Prophecy.

What makes the Scriptures absolute is that when it was being collated, the entire theme was centered on one Man: Jesus Christ. (John 5:39-47). So, to understand the subject of tithing, we are not just going to look at it as the passage, we will have to subject it to the interpretation of the Gospels and the Epistles. What did Jesus say about tithing? How do the Epistles address the subject of tithing?

It's interesting to note that the word tithe, tithing, or to tithe are words that were not emphasized in the Epistles. In fact, the word was only used once by the writer of Hebrews, and it was not an instruction but a historical reference. Hebrews 7:5-9 reads, *"And verily they that are of the sons of Levi, who receive the priesthood, have a commandment to take tithes from the people according to the law, that is, of their brethren, though they have come from the loins of Abraham: But he whose descent is not counted from them received tithes from Abraham, and blessed him that had the promises. And without all contradiction the less is blessed of the better. And here men that die receive tithes; but there he receiveth them, of whom it is witnessed that he liveth. And as I may so say, Levi also, who receieth tithes, paid tithes in Abraham. "*

Now, the account referred to by the author of the book of Hebrews can be found in Genesis 14:17-23, and we shall look at it shortly. This is the only reference to tithing you will see throughout the Epistles.

The writer of the book of Hebrews was not encouraging people to tithe in these verses any more than Hebrews 11:17 was an encouragement to offer your sons just as Abraham did. There are lessons to learn from historical accounts, but some have tried to create a doctrine out of the Hebrews' singular mention of the tithe.

They claim verse 8 means Jesus received tithe. This is unscriptural and certainly not true. The phrase "he received them" is italicized in the English text. This means that the phrase was not in the original text. Rather, it was added by the translators, in this case the King James translators since we are quoting from the King James Bible. A contextual reading will plainly show the reader he was referring to Melchizedek symbolically. (*See* Hebrews 7:3).

How was tithing taught in the New Testament books of the Bible?

The words "tithe" or "to tithe" or "tithing" were not mentioned at all in the book of Acts, not mentioned in the Pauline Epistles, nor in Peter, John, James, or Jude's Epistles. This pattern of its lack of mention in the New Testament writings is very instructive, as all the Apostles taught giving, but none taught the tithe or tithing.

Firstly, let us examine what Jesus Christ said about the tithe. Jesus spoke about the tithe twice: once as rebuke and once in a parable.

As a rebuke:

Mathew 23:23 reads, "Woe to you, scribes and Pharisees, hypocrites! For you pay tithe of mint and anise and cummin and have neglected the weightier matters of the law: justice and mercy and faith. These you ought to have done, without leaving the others undone.").

Jesus expressly refers to the tithe as a matter of the law, same as mercy, judgment, and faithfulness. So, Jesus was not instructing tithing here, as tithing preceded his incarnation. That is, these customs were already in practice before the advent of Jesus Christ's coming.

Just like other practices like Passover, Pentecost, and all the ceremonial sacrifices, they all preceded Jesus Christ's coming. Who was Jesus' audience here? The Pharisees and the scribes (the religious sects).

As a parable:

Luke 18:11-12 reads, *"The Pharisee stood and prayed thus with himself, 'God, I thank You that I am not as other men – extortioners, unjust, adulterers, or even as this tax collector. I fast twice in the week, I give tithes of all that I possess."*

It's notable to see that the speaker is a Pharisee yet again. Thus, on the two occasions where Jesus mentioned the tithe, he was not commending the tither. In fact, if you read these verses in context (verses 13-14), He talks about the pride of this Pharisee. So, we have two mentions by Jesus, which are rebuking and exposing the hypocrisy of the Pharisees, and one mention in the Epistles, which is historical and not an instruction.

The Epistles are the explanation of the Old Testament books of the Bible. Hence being emphatic that tithe will not be following through with the Epistles concerning how giving was taught. This then leads us to a very important question: Is the nonpayment of tithe robbing God? This ideology has its origin in a text in the Old Testament:

Malachi 3:6-10 reads, *"For I am the LORD, I change not; therefore, ye sons of Jacob are not consumed. Even from the days of your fathers ye are gone away from mine ordinances, and have not kept them. Return unto me, and I will return unto you, saith the LORD of hosts. But ye said, Wherein shall we return? Will a man rob God? Yet ye have robbed me. But ye say, Wherein have we robbed thee? In tithes and offerings. Ye are cursed with a curse: for ye have robbed me, even this whole nation. Bring ye all the tithes into the storehouse, that there may be meat in mine house, and prove me now herewith, saith the LORD of hosts, if I will not open you the windows of heaven, and pour you out a blessing, that there shall not be room enough to receive it."* Malachi 3:6-10

The prophet Malachi spoke about bringing the tithe into the store house, observed from the law of Moses in Numbers 18:25-32. In Numbers 18, God was telling the Levites to take out 10% from whatever produce they may have collected from the Israelites. Did you get that? The Levites.

So, the people who were to bring the 10%, as seen in the book of Numbers 18, were the Levites. Who are the Levites? The Levites were one of the tribes of Israel who did nothing but attend to the Tabernacle (Temple) and the spiritual needs of the nation of Israel. Because they did not do anything else – they did not farm or do any other job –

the entire nation of Israel was asked to pay a tithe to them from their harvest, crops, and livestock. That was considered the Levites' reward or wages since they worked in the Temple.

Moses instructed that the Levites take a tithe from the children of Israel as their inheritance. They were instructed to also offer up a tenth of that tithe unto the Lord as their heave offering. Nehemiah also spoke about the tithe in Nehemiah 13:10-14.

The golden question is who then was the prophet Malachi referring to in Malachi 3? I'd like you to note that Malachi, Zachariah, and Haggai all spoke about the Temple. They came chronologically after Nehemiah, so everything they said was in the same dispensation. This was when they were back from the exile. (*See* Nehemiah 13:4-13).

Nehemiah 13:4-13 shows that they were restoring the practice of the Levites and the priesthood after returning from exile because at that time, the tithe was restricted to the promised land, Canaan. Now, a basic fact that must be established is who was the book of Malachi written to?

In Malachi 1:6, the first audience was the priests, and this is consistent throughout the book of Malachi. (Malachi 2:1 & 3:3). The instructions contained in the book of Malachi were to the Levites. They are the ones that brought the tithe into the storehouse but in verse of Malachi 3 the audience switched to the people.

Now, observe carefully in verses 8-10. "*Will a man rob God? Yet ye have robbed me. But ye say, wherein have we robbed thee? In tithes and offerings. Ye are cursed with a curse: for ye have robbed me, even this whole nation. Bring ye all the tithes into the storehouse, that there may be meat in mine house, and prove me now herewith, saith the Lord of hosts, if I will not open you the door of heaven, and pour you out a blessing, that there may not be room enough to receive it."*

Now, did you observe the phrase "even this whole nation"? That is indicative that the first audience and the main audience of Malachi was the priests. Why? Because the prophet Malachi introduced the entire nation of Israel as victims of the priests' refusal to bring in their tithe as instructed by Moses.

It's evident that the key thing Malachi was addressing here was selfishness: The word "meat" was translated from the word *tereph* in the Hebrew lexicon. It majorly refers to leaves, like vegetarian food, though it includes other kinds of foods. Thus "the tithe" was not money but plants and livestock. Meat refers to food. There is no other interpretation. That is what the Scriptures call it, and that is exactly what it says. It's food. Not dollars, pounds, or naira but food. Plants and livestock.

The word "store" was translated from the Hebrew word *otsar*, which means a treasury, a safe place where they kept food. The word storehouse (*otsar*) was also mentioned in Deuteronomy 28:12, Deuteronomy 32:34, and 1 Kings 7:51. The *ostar* is built in such a way that it can preserve food. It was not Bank of America, Capital One, Wells Fargo, First Bank, or Zenith Bank. It was a wooden- and mud-built silo.

The word "house" was translated from the word *bayeith*. It means a temple. These words were used literally and referred to physical things. The period the tithes were brought in was the same period the priests were present to minister on behalf of the nation, and because the Levites were part of that ministry and did not farm or labor like the other tribes, they had no food to eat. The Israelites would bring food for the priests in the temple. Everything is physically explained.

The word "rob" was translated from the Hebrew word *qaba*, which means to cheat someone of something that is his/hers. It was the same word used in Proverbs 22:23, translated as "spoil." Thus to "rob" means to spoil, to circumvent, and cheat. It means not to give another what is deserved. It's different from the word used to describe a criminal or a thief. A thief is one that breaks in to steal or take something not belonging to him/her. These are two different things.

In other words, Malachi meant that the Levites were not bringing the tithes, which was food to the store house, since they were the ones that brought the food into the storehouse in the tabernacle. So, robbing God was in reference to the Levites cheating the priests or depriving the priests who served in the temple of what was rightfully theirs. This instruction was therefore not for the believer.

Is it therefore wrong to tithe?

Note that the word "tithe" means to give a tenth (10%) of your income or earnings etc. Hence, since it is yours, then it certainly cannot be wrong. However, the question to ask is this:

Is it mandatory to tithe your income?

Obviously, since there are no such instructions in the New Testament, whoever makes people do so is not instructing from the Scriptures, therefore the answer is NO. Any pastor/bishop who is asking people to tithe mandatorily, however mightily placed he/she is in Christendom, is going against the Scriptures. Notice, however, that a key lesson one might fail to see is that the tithe was done to honor God at different points in people's lives.

---

*Tithing is an Old Testament
law requirement, like Pentecost and Passover.*

The first tithers in the Bible: Abraham and Jacob

ABRAHAM:

Abraham, the friend of God, was the first to ever tithe as seen from the scriptures. Genesis 14:19-20 reads, *"And he blessed him, and said, Blessed be Abram of the most high God, possessor of heaven and earth: And blessed be the most high God, which hath delivered thine enemies into thy hand. And he gave him tithes of all."*

Nobody instructed Abraham to pay tithe, not God or any prophet. The patriarch Abraham went to war, and when he came back from a victorious battle, he saw Melchizedek the priest, and the joy of winning the battle provoked Abraham to take 10% of the spoils of war and willingly "give," not "pay." He gave because it was not an obligation. He generously gave out of joy. Nobody preached to him to pay or be cursed; nobody preached to him to pay if he wanted to be blessed, no. Abraham gave voluntarily.

JACOB:

Jacob was the second person to tithe as noticed from the scriptures. Genesis 28:20-22 reads, *"And Jacob vowed a vow, saying, If God will be with me, and will keep me in this way that I go, and will give me bread to eat, and raiment to put on, So that I come again to my father's house in peace; then shall the LORD be my God: And this stone, which I have set for a pillar, shall be God's house: and of all that thou shalt give me I will surely give the tenth unto thee."*

Jacob did the same thing as Abraham. Jacob poured oil on a stone in Genesis and said, "God if you take me and bring me back, I will give 10%," not "I will pay." Nobody instructed Jacob to pay or give. God never instructed Jacob or Abraham to pay or give tithe. It was Jacob's choice to do so. Jacob made the vow to tithe if God blessed him.

The two scenarios show tithes as an honor to God from whom all blessings came. Also, it's noteworthy that both Abraham and Jacob did this once. Throughout the Old Testament, there were no other mentions of Abraham or Jacob tithing again.

Are you cursed if you refuse to pay tithe?

Of course, that is a capital NO. *"There is therefore now no condemnation to them who are in Christ Jesus."* (Romans 8:1a). Jesus Christ has redeemed you from the law being made a curse for you. (*See* Galatians 3:12-14).

Let us examine the Old Testament (the law) on tithing. There are several texts on tithing in the law. However, the following is very instructive. Deuteronomy 14:28-29 reads, *"At the end of three years thou shalt bring forth all the tithe of thine increase the same year, and shalt lay it up within thy gates: And the Levite, (because he hath no part nor inheritance with thee,) and the stranger, and the fatherless, and the widow, which are within thy gates, shall come, and shall eat and be satisfied; that the LORD thy God may bless thee in all the work of thine hand which thou doest."*

We can see from Deuteronomy 14 that the tithes were meant for the following persons:

1. The Levites: Why? The Levites were priests, who were not allowed to have an inheritance in the promised land – no farm, no livestock, no real estate or business. Their job was to serve in the temple of the Lord and attend to the spiritual needs of the Israelites. Hence the need for the Israelites to support them with food. (*See* Numbers 18:20-21).

Since the Levites were to be at the service of the people, they had to be taken care of by the people. In the Epistles, Paul equates this to New Testament ministers saying: *"Do ye not know that they which minister about holy things live of the things of the temple? and they which wait at the altar are partakers with the altar? Even so hath the Lord ordained that they which preach the gospel should live of the gospel."* (1 Corinthians 9:13-14).

Notice, Paul never asked believers to give them (ministers, i.e. pastors, bishops, or prophets) tithes. Rather, the church was to support them materially, and no percentage was given. We are instructed to care for our pastors and ministers. Be it pastors, bishops, or whatever title.

We are instructed to care for our church leaders generously, but no percentage is given. So, the choice is yours to make, whether it be groceries, 1% or 100%. (*See* 1 Timothy 5:17-18).

If a man of God is laboring in the vineyard, he is entitled to double wages. We are expected to care for and give to that man of God handsomely and not just casual handouts. Galatians 6:6 (NASB) reads, *"The one who is taught the word is to share all good things with the one who teaches him."* (The term "good things" implies things of value and not just anything you feel like. In other words, our pastors must be well taken care of.

Again, notice that the word "tithe" was not used, neither was there a percentage for the gifts. Rather, wages, reward, or good things. Why is this so? Paul had taught how to give in his letters. (*See* 2 Corinthians 9:7). From Paul's explanation, you (the believer/church member) are to decide what wages or good things you give to support for your pastors. This must not be done grudgingly, because ministers ought to be well cared for.

This refers to support and caring for their needs and not appetites. Owning private jets is an appetite; luxurious mansions are appetites; Ferraris and Lamborghinis are appetites and not needs. Why should you give your money to a church were the pastors own private jets and live in million dollar luxurious mansions while there are servants of God in remote villages and communities who needs that help to continue the work of the ministry? Why?

2. Strangers, widows and fatherless, the poor/needy folks among us (Malachi 3:5). *"For it hath pleased them of Macedonia and Achaia to make a certain contribution for the poor saints which are at Jerusalem."* (Romans 15:26). We can see that the church in Macedonia collected a contribution and sent the entire amount to the poor and needy people in Jerusalem. (*See* 1 Corinthians 16:1-2; James 1:27; Acts 4:32-35; Acts 6:1-4).

The tithes of the Old Testament law were meant for this category of brethren. Today, our giving is for pastors, church members who are poor, and those who need support like school fees, medical emergencies, or in times like the global pandemic of Coronavirus. This giving is meant to honor God, and our giving should always reflect that. (*See* Proverbs 3:9).

No Christian should find it difficult to honor God with his or her income or services. However, it must be clear that there must be no mandatory percentage foisted on anyone.

It's key to note that Paul gave instructions on how to give. 1 Corinthians 16:2 Paul said, *"Upon the first day of the week let every one of you lay by him in store, as God hath prospered him, that there be no gatherings when I come."* Observe that the word "God" was italicized, which implies it was inserted by the translators. Thus, the text can be better understood as: "Upon the first day of the week let every one of you lay by him in store as he has prospered, that there be no gatherings when I come." In other words, as one prospers, let him/her give. That is, your giving should be proportional to your income. Notice again, Paul did not mention the tithe or any percentage. He need not use percentages for men and women born of the Spirit.

New covenant believers don't give
because they want to be blessed.
They give because they are already blessed in Jesus.

So, are you cursed if you refused to pay tithe? Of course, that is a capital NO. No believer is cursed. (*See* Galatians 3:12-14). You are blessed and will always remain blessed. God has blessed you with all you need in life. Do not allow any pastor to tell you different.

God doesn't bless you because you tithe and won't curse you because you don't. God doesn't want you to tithe, but God expects us to give to those around us who are poor, sick, and need our help. God expects you to show love to the less privileged, the orphans, the widows, the fatherless, and the older population around us. God expects us to be the good Samaritan to that stranger on our path or in our community. (*See* Mathew 25:35-40).

Give to support your local churches. Give so your church can continue preaching the gospel to you and to the world, doing the missionary works they do, and paying all the staff working in the church. But let it be a church support offering or pastor support. This is a "voluntarily" obligation to your local church. Don't give because you want God to bless you. Give because God has blessed you and because you want to honor God with your resources.

Religion has given birth to all manner of false doctrines and money grabbing masters who are after people's bank account and not the growth of the believers, men who fly private jets and live in mansions at the expense of their ignorant congregation.

Any country whose citizens pay more tithes than taxes will always borrow and depend on a country whose citizens pays more tax than tithe.

Any country whose citizens pay more tithes than taxes will always borrow and depend on a country whose citizens pay more tax than tithe. This is the problem facing a lot of African Countries. Religion has produced more fraud than politics.

The greatest fraud is being committed in some Pentecostal churches of today on broad daylight, and no one is saying anything because these religious Mafias are hiding behind the pulpit and collar to brainwash and extort from the saints. These pastors' own houses all over the world, some own private universities with tuitions even more expensive than government universities and colleges. There are some schools owned by some of this churches that even members of the church cannot afford to attend. Some have five-star hotels, shipping companies, and even hold shares in multi-national corporations all over the world.

How did they make all this money? Is it not from their church members? Many of these pastors had nothing before they went into the ministry. Do you know how much these pastors make from these tithes? Imagine 10% of the income of one hundred members. Now imagine what that figure will be for a church with 10 to 30 thousand members. This is why we have many people rushing to open their own churches and the reason why we have more churches than industries in many African countries, specifically Nigeria

When other nations are building industries and establishing companies, many African countries, especially my country Nigeria, are busy opening more and more churches on every corner of the street. Nigeria has the largest church auditorium in the world. Big church buildings and edifices without industries and companies. How can such a country thrive and compete with developed nations of the world?

Nigeria is a developing country with a GDP (Gross Domestic Product) of less than 400 billion dollars, but this same country has the richest pastors in the world. Isn't that surprising? I am not against ministers living a good life, far from it. I believe men of God should live decent lives but not amass wealth at the expense of their members.

Church has become a business and one of the fast avenues to unchecked and untaxed wealth. Gone are the days when men went into ministry for the sake of the gospel of salvation. Now it's for the sake of their bank accounts. Is this the kind of ministry Apostle Paul did? Did the disciples live the kind of lavish lifestyles we see among some pastors of today? Did the Apostle Paul have a private ship, boat, or even donkey? Did Jesus Christ or Apostle Paul live in luxurious mansions while on earth?

Somehow, I feel as though "Pentecostalism" have created room for wolves, for fraudsters, and Juju priests to enter the Church of Jesus Christ who are bent on enriching themselves and their families at the expense of the congregation. There is a wave of spiritual awakening sweeping through Christendom and soon, these money chasers will go out of business as their devices and ploys are gradually exposed. Their fake prophecies that never comes to pass, their fear driven hell fire and Satan-centered teachings are coming to an end.

The good news of the death, burial, and resurrection of Jesus Christ and His love for the world and the gift of righteousness is gradually taking central stage in many churches as it was meant to be. All over the world, people are awakening to their new life of grace, their rights and privileges in Jesus Christ. The truth is prevailing, and nothing can stop it.

Demystifying Fasting in light of the New Testament

Fasting is a practice that spans through the whole of Scripture. However, there is fasting as was done in the Old Testament and there is New Testament fasting. What do I mean?

We don't fast to receive from God.
We fast as a means of consecration
and fellowship with God.

People fasted in the Old Testament for many reasons. They fasted because they wanted to seek God's face. They fasted for forgiveness of sins (e.g. tearing of clothes and putting on sackcloth and ashes in order to seek the forgiveness of God).

They fasted when they felt like they were under a curse or they felt like the heavens were shut towards them (e.g. in the Old Testament you see a Prophet say: if my people who are called by my name shall humble themselves and fast and pray, and turn from their wicked ways and seek my face, I will hear from heaven. But this was the prophet's opinion.) They also fasted to seek for God's intervention in war between countries and fasted to seek material things.

We also saw Moses and Elijah, who both fasted for 40 days to seek God's face...but when Jesus fasted for 40 days, it was not for the same reason as Moses and Elijah, but rather to prepare Himself, through prayer and fellowship with His Father, for His assignment.

The New Testament Church begins after Pentecost...In the New Testament we don't fast to seek the face of God because God dwells in us. We don't fast to seek for forgiveness because we are forgiven by the sacrificial work of Christ.

The reason for Fasting in the Old Testament is totally different from that of the New Testament.

We don't fast to seek for freedom from curses because Jesus had redeemed us from the curse. (Galatians 3:13). We also do not fast to get things, because His divine power has granted to us everything pertaining to life and godliness. (2 Peter 1:3, NASB).

New Testament Pattern of Prayer

It's important that you understand the concept of prayer and how to make effective use of it in order to maximize its benefits in your life. Prayer is a very profound means of relationship and intimacy with God. Prayer is not the means for you to ask God for anything, but rather it's a way through which you receive by faith those things that have been made available to you.

Through prayer, a believer enforces spiritual power against the enemy. Through prayer, we get to go into a spiritual intercourse with God. A key thing to note in the New Testament pattern of prayer is that it was done with gratitude in one's heart. You go into prayer with gratitude that what you need has been made available for you.

Grace doesn't exclude a believer from praying because prayer is a way to exercise sonship or your rights in the kingdom. We don't pray to ask; we go to prayer to receive what has been provided to us through Jesus Christ. The errors I have seen in many of the prayers we offer today in churches and in our homes is that we pray outside of the knowledge of the significance of the new covenant and lack of understanding of the Scriptures.

The prayer is the receiving. The moment you start praying, that is the same moment you start receiving or taking delivery of your answers. God doesn't hold back; He has provided all you need. Remember that your prayer doesn't move God, nor does God reacts to your prayer. God acted before you prayed.

It's also imperative that you are aware that you don't have a faith problem as a believer. When you feel like you lack faith, and as a result, your prayers are not answered, you are acting/judging from a point of ignorance. No believer has a lack of faith problem.

What some believers lack is inability to exercise faith. Why? Faith is also a gift or one of the contents of the package of redemption. Romans 12:3 reads; *"For by the grace given me I say to every one of you: Do not think of yourself more highly than you ought, but rather think of yourself with sober judgment, in accordance with the faith God has distributed to each of you."* (ESV).

Faith has already been given unto you, so exercise it. The finished work of Jesus Christ was a complete package. It comes with all the believer needs to fully enjoy his or her new life. The new covenant life was designed in such a way that Man has no part in its achievement but is instead a beneficiary of it.

As a new covenant believer, there is no role you played in the attainment of your redemption. The new covenant closed all avenues that would give you the opportunity to boast. In this new covenant living, our boasting or pride is not in ourselves but in the person of Jesus Christ, His triumph through His death and resurrection on our behalf.

We have been wrongly taught that until we pray, God doesn't answer or that it's when we pray that God answers. I'd like you to know that in Jesus Christ, all prayers have been answered. In Jesus Christ, all needs of Man have been provided. The day you became born again; you also received the answers for all you will ever need. So, through prayers you collect those things or take possession of them.

Prayer is reasoning with God on the platform of His word. It's a medium through which you exercise your authority and dominion on earth as was given to you at creation. (*See* Genesis 1:26-28). Prayer must be done around the character and nature of God. What do I mean by this? When you pray and ask God to kill someone who did you wrong, or you pray to ask God to hurt or punish someone who hurt you, such prayer is not in line with the character and nature of God. Asking God to kill someone or hurt them is a foolish prayer point. God doesn't kill or hurt people. It's not in His nature.

Also, certain kinds of prayers Christians pray, especially in developing nations like my country of birth Nigeria, are because of a failed economy and government. When you live in a developed nation where the economy is good and the government is making efficient use of taxpayer's money, certain kinds of prayer requests will leave your mouth.

You don't need Jesus or prayer to make money or have certain material things. If you did, then people of other religions who do not believe in Jesus Christ would all be poor and helpless, but you and I know that is not the case. When you have a thriving economy, and low unemployment rate, and the good skills/ education needed you get job offers easily.

If there are good roads all through your country, you are more confidents as long as you are obeying all traffic rules and regulations. You don't necessarily start panicking and speaking in tongues and praying for safety on the road because the road is safe to a large extent. But if you are living in a corrupt country were the roads are bad and dangerous, of course your instinct as a Christian is to always pray consistently out of fear each time you are travelling.

For example, a job candidate in the United States or any Western country is different from a job candidate in Nigeria or Cameroon. Why? because the environment is different. A job applicant in Cameroon, will have to have a good University degree and graduate with first class or second class and then do well in the interview. Even when this job applicant is qualified, there is the problem of corruption which manifests in various ways.

For a man, he must know someone to get the job. For the ladies, they are asked for sex or some form of relationship. So if you're a Christian living in a country were experience and qualification is for the most part second to connection, seeing that you don't have any political connection or know someone who can help speak on your behalf to get the job, all you can do is to go into an unnecessary 7 days of fasting and prayer, blaming all the witches in your community, your grandparents or a family curse as the reason for your predicament or the reason for not getting the job. Whereas it's the result of a failed and corrupt government.

Not everything is resolved through prayer. You must differentiate between those things that are happening or affecting you as a result of a failed economy and corrupt government from those that are spiritual. Being a Christian or believer doesn't exclude you from the effects of a poor economy or bad and corrupt government. Therefore, you need sound spiritual and physical knowledge.

In many African countries, Christians pray about everything, and we think it's right or normal but it's not. We pray about money as though money falls from heaven. They pray for a visa to travel abroad. I myself made this same mistake. I remember how I was fasting and praying just because I wanted to get a visa to travel to a Western country many years ago. A prayer of foolishness and ignorance.

Does a British citizen pray and fast for visa to travel to any African country, or any European, Asian or American country? I don't think so. I have never gone to any church in the United States or the United Kingdom and heard members give testimony of how God answered their prayers and gave him/her a visa to an African or European nation. That's is not something you testify about or treasure like a golden egg.

If not for business or tourism and experiencing the world, there is no reason for an American, German, or British citizen, even citizens of UAE, to travel to any country for anything. Why do I say so? Because all he or she needs is available in his/her country. There is good education, job opportunities with good salaries, security, good roads, a good healthcare system, and a working government.

If you go to many churches in Nigeria, there is no Sunday service were people don't give testimony for visas or where the pastor doesn't include getting visas to travel to a Western nation as the favor and rare blessing of God for those who are faithful and pays their tithes. Some pastors even have special anointing service for people looking for visas to travel abroad as though it's a divine achievement or benefit.

If these countries were as successful as the United States or other developed nations like the UK, Germany, or Canada, why would their citizens, including my humble self, leave our motherland for greener pastures elsewhere?

A country with high unemployment rate, low wages, poor Healthcare facilities, and no constant Electricity supply... Why wouldn't people pray about virtually everything? Why wouldn't people be afraid of armed robbers and kidnappers while traveling? The same kidnappers and armed robbers are citizens who are acting out of frustration due to lack of job and means to survive.

To pray effectively, one must have a sound knowledge of the nature and personality of God, the significance of the finished works of Jesus Christ, and most importantly, one must be conscious of his restored identity in Christ. Effective and fervent prayer is not in the loudness of your voice or the use of large vocabularies, tongue speaking, or the duration you pray. A prayer is effective when it's done in knowledge and backed up by faith.

In Jesus Christ, all your prayers/needs have been answered and provided.

It's your duty to receive or enforce it. This is where prayer comes in. This knowledge is very important if you want to pray effectively.

Do you need healing? Then go into prayer and receive it by faith. Note, I said receive not ask. Do you need wisdom in any area of your life? Then go into prayer and receive it by faith. Do you need the fruit of the womb? Then go into prayer and receive it by faith. Do you need ideas for financial breakthroughs? Then go into prayer and receive it by faith. Do you need protection over your life and that of your loved ones? Then go into prayer and receive it by faith.

Faith is the tool through which we receive what grace has provided. Our prayer must come out of a heart of gratitude first. Gratitude for what? Gratitude for the gift of salvation, gratitude for the forgiveness of sins, gratitude for eternal life, and gratitude for what you are about to receive.

In the New Testament, unlike the Old, we show gratitude before we receive, not after we had received. Why? Because we are conscious of the fact that it was provided even before we came to know and confess Jesus as our only Lord and Savior.

In Jesus Christ, all your prayers/needs
have been answered and provided,
It's your duty to receive or enforce it.

So why do we fast in the New Testament?

We fast as an act of consecration, to set ourselves apart so we can pray and fellowship with God without any interruption. Fasting in the New Testament was also done when there was a need to set people apart for Ministry (e.g. In Acts 13...they ministered unto the lord in fasting, and the Holy Ghost said, "separate unto me Paul and Barnabas.")

These are the reasons why we fast in the New Testament. Back home I did a teaching on fasting, and I said: Fasting doesn't have to be 6am to 6pm. It can be 6pm to 6am. The important thing is that you spend time fellowshipping and enjoying your father presence, through prayer, worship songs or even studying the word of God.

Fasting without these three activities prayer, word studying and worship to me. is simply a hunger strike.

Most people who work during the day don't have the time to pray...it's pointless if you are going to fast without praying. You are simply punishing your body. For such people you should eat well in the day and fast at night, pray, and study. There is no stipulated time fixed for fasting.

Fasting without prayer, worship or Bible study is simply a hunger strike.

It is not the punishing of our bodies that is the fasting, but the time spent to pray and study or just simply fellowshipping with the father, away from all distractions. If you have a serious problem you can also take a fast...it is not the fast as an act that solves your problem, but in the place of fasting, praying, and fellowship, God gives you wisdom and direction on how to overcome the problem.

CHAPTER 14

WHY YOU CAN DROP YOUR CROSS AND TAKE UP HIS GLORY

The subtitle of this book reads; "Why you can break out of the prison of religion, drop your cross, take up His glory and start enjoying your new life In Christ." Dropping your cross may sound kind of ambiguous to a religious and legalistic mind due to the statement in one of the four gospels. Let's look at that Scripture in Mathew 16:24 (NIV). It reads, *"Then Jesus said to his disciples, 'Whoever wants to be my disciple must deny themselves and take up their cross and follow me.'"* This statement has been wrongly applied to New Testament believers, which ought not to be. Some folks have maintained that a born-again believer needs to carry his cross daily.

The "cross" symbolizes sufferings, burdens, or penalties. What was Jesus referring to when he said cross in Mathew 16? Are we expected to still be carrying our crosses around till death? Why am I saying you should drop your cross and take up His glory?

As I said in previous chapters, the four synoptic gospels (Mathew, Mark, Luke and John) are considered transitional Scriptures. They are not the beginning of the New Testament because Jesus was still very much alive. The death and resurrection of Jesus ushered in the new testament or new covenant or new birth and new life.

When Jesus made that statement in Mathew 16:24, He was referring to our inclusion in His death and resurrection. So, when He told His disciples to carry their cross and follow Him, He was speaking of His death and resurrection. Remember that before Christ's death and resurrection, we had our crosses on our own heads. We carried our crosses which symbolized our death, the weight of sin, guilt, condemnation, works, and self-reliance. But none of us went to the cross except Jesus Christ. Jesus took all our crosses upon Himself. He took all our burdens, the weight of sins, the condemnation, the guilt, the old man and went up to the cross and died with it.

But Great, didn't Jesus have just one cross on Him? Yes, my friend, He did. But that one cross represented all of us. That one cross that He carried contained you and me – our individual crosses. That is how powerful and lethal Jesus Christ's finished work is to any person who through faith, receives Him in their life.

When you believe and accept by faith the finished work of Jesus into your heart, you don't need to continue carrying your cross because He has carried it for you. Your cross became His own. What you are expected to take up is His glory, the benefit of His death and resurrection, the victory, and the new and sweet beautiful life in Him.

Note that when Jesus gave this instruction to His disciples, He had not died yet. Therefore, His disciples where still unbelievers. No one was righteous before the death of Jesus Christ, not even the disciples, since they were all still living under the law.

The law cannot make any man righteous. The cross belongs to Jesus, not you. "Carrying the cross" was Jesus's assignment. The cross was the work of Jesus Christ, but by Faith it became ours. So, when Jesus told His disciples to take up their cross, He was asking them to take Him up.

Jesus was asking His disciples to receive Him, to do away with their ability to keep the law, to let go of "self" and receive the new life in Him which was about to be ushered in through His resurrection.

Colossians 2:14 (NIV) reads, *"Having canceled the charge of our legal indebtedness, which stood against us and condemned us; he has taken it away, nailing it to his cross."* The King James version rendered it this way: *"Blotting out the handwriting of ordinances that was against us, which was contrary to us, and took it out of the way, nailing it to his cross."*

Notice how it says "his cross" in both the NIV and KJV versions? That says a lot. Friend, the finished work of Jesus Christ took care of your cross So, drop your cross and take up His life. God did not do an incomplete job. God cannot say you are redeemed and still want you to carry your cross of the burden and weight of sin. Jesus' death and resurrection has taken care of your cross.

His Sacrifice Was Enough

Easter is the time of year when we celebrate the death, burial, and resurrection of our Lord Jesus Christ. Some Easter celebrations are simple, like flying kites or eating hot cross buns or lighting bonfires. Others, however, are more on the extreme side.

Some cultures celebrate by wearing bizarre costumes or staging a fireworks battle. Others burn effigies of Judas Iscariot. In some places, animal sacrifice is a common practice. Elsewhere, self-flagellation — whipping oneself is not unheard of. People will carry heavy religious objects to show their devotion. During some reenactments of Jesus' crucifixion, the actors playing Jesus will wear genuine crowns of thorns and carry weighty crosses.

Why do people do such things? It may be because they want others to understand what Jesus experienced. But most do these things in the name of penance. They are trying to atone for the wrong they have done, and they're using religious means to do it.

While the Scriptures do tell us that we are crucified with Christ, that's not meant in a literal sense. We don't have to be physically crucified like Jesus was. His sacrifice was enough. And that's what a lot of people miss. Our acts of penance, or self-punishment, for our sins are unnecessary. In fact, they're as much an offense to God as sin is. We cannot atone for ourselves. We cannot appease God's wrath.

The whole first part of Hebrews 10 talks about how the sacrifices made in the Old Testament weren't enough to save people. Hebrews 10:4 reads: *"For it is not possible that the blood of bulls and of goats should take away sins".* But that same chapter also tells us that *"by one offering [Jesus] hath perfected forever them that are sanctified."* (Hebrews 10:14). The repeated offerings of bulls and goats couldn't remove sin, but one offering by Jesus was more than enough.

Jesus did more than satisfy the debt of sin. Nothing can be added to His sacrifice. It can't be improved upon. Man is an improvement addict; we like to improve everything from cell phones to automobiles to fashion and even life itself. Recently a laboratory has announced work on creating a genetically enhance human that is able to fly, and do everything machines can do.

Today we have iPhone 11 pro max, Galaxy s20 plus and just one month into this new product, both Apple and Samsung, have announced new higher versions of these flagship Phones. But folks there is no improvement or higher version of Jesus Christ's finished works on the cross, He said its finished, the veil is torn, nothing more nothing less. So, if He paid it all, there's nothing left for us to pay. Acts of penance are pointless. All they do is say that what Jesus did wasn't enough.

The veil is torn friend. Any message that says otherwise is the message of the Anti-Christ. In my years of service in the church, I discovered that most people's image of the Anti-Christ is a beast with two tusks or an alien from hell with a red tail and sharp claws, but that is not the case. Yes, that might be what he looks like in movies, but the real Anti-Christs are here already in flesh and blood, living in our communities. Some are colleagues at work, classmates, friends, and even family members.

Who is antichrist? An antichrist is a person who is against the finished work of Jesus on the cross, a person who has opted for his own way of salvation instead of the one that has been freely provided to us by Jesus Christ. Anti-Christs are simply against Christ and what He has done through His death and resurrection.

The cross was not a down payment on the sin debt and now we have to make monthly payments on the balance. No! There's no debt left! And the sooner we realize that and start living our lives based on that knowledge, the better off we'll be. We can't live our New Testament lives with an Old Testament mindset. All those sacrifices in the Old Testament kept people aware of their sins. But praise God that we have been set free. We have been translated into a new kingdom where God no longer remembers our sins (Hebrew 10:17).

We can't live our New Testament lives with an Old Testament mindset.

We have to choose whether we're going to live by works or by the grace Jesus has provided (Romans 11:6). Of course, we know that works won't achieve salvation. This is a multiple-choice question, and we already have the answer. Trying to add to Jesus' accomplished work is like finger-painting on the Mona Lisa—we're just ruining a masterpiece. We need to step back into God's way of doing things and trust in His plan.

The War Is Over and You Won in Christ

Do you remember September 11, 2001 (9/11)? Of course, you do. If you've lived very long, you can recall many terrible things that have happened in this world, including tsunamis and hurricanes of biblical proportions. And certainly, each one of you has your own individual tragedy that you deal with or have dealt with. There is a lot of hurt and pain in this life.

People are reeling from the blows they've received and are trying to make sense of why all of this happens. Sadly, many Christian leaders haven't been much help. As a whole, they've said these things are the judgment of God upon our sins.

Even a very well-known televangelist was quoted recently telling people that God was using the coronavirus to judge the whole world for sins. Some said God was cleansing the earth through the coronavirus for its many abominations like homosexuality and abortions. This rationale for why bad things happen grieves me, and I believe it grieves the Lord too.

It's totally missing the point of why Jesus came. Jesus forever changed the way God relates to mankind. Sure, there are Scriptural examples of God's catastrophic judgment on sin. But God's greatest act of judgment was when He placed all His wrath for our sins upon Jesus. This forever satisfied God's wrath. Since that time, God hasn't been judging our sins (2 Corinthians 5:19).

God's not angry at us. He's not even in a bad mood. Look at the angels' joy at the birth of Jesus in Bethlehem. Luke 2:13-14 says, *"And suddenly there was with the angel a multitude of the heavenly host praising God, and saying,*

Glory to God in the highest, and on earth peace, good will toward men."

This scripture is very familiar to us, yet there is a lot of misunderstanding about what it's saying. Some translations say they were proclaiming "good will among men" or "peace to men of good will." Basically, this passage has been interpreted to say Jesus was bringing peace on earth among people. That's not why these angels were praising God. If that interpretation were true, then Jesus' own words in Matthew 10:34-36 would contradict this. He said, *"Think not that I am come to send peace on earth: I came not to send peace, but a sword. For I am come to set a man at variance against his father, and the daughter against her mother, and the daughter in law against her mother in law. And a man's foes shall be they of his own household."*

Jesus Himself said He was not sent to bring peace on the earth among people. The peace that the angels of Luke 2:13-14 were praising God for was peace between God and Man. They were announcing the end of God's war on sin. Peace now reigns between God and Man.

Prior to Jesus' coming, there was wrath from God against mankind for his sins. It wasn't total wrath. Even in the Old Testament, we see God's mercy and grace. The Old Testament Law was a ministry of wrath (Romans 4:15 & 2 Corinthians 3:7-9), and people's sins were held against them. But when Jesus came, God quit holding people's sins against them. This is exactly what 2 Corinthians says: *"To wit, that God was in Christ, reconciling the world unto himself, not imputing their trespasses unto them; and hath committed unto us the word of reconciliation...For he hath made him to be sin for us, who knew no sin; that we might be made the righteousness of God in him."* (2 Corinthians 5:19,21).

The word "reconciliation" is about making peace. God was no longer holding us accountable. Instead, He imputed our sins to Jesus, making Jesus accountable for our sins. Jesus became what we were so we could become what He was—the righteousness of God.

Jesus was like a lightning rod that drew all the judgment of God unto Himself. He not only bore our sins; He actually became sin (2 Corinthians 5:21). Jesus said this: *"Now is my soul troubled; and what shall I say? Father, save me from this hour: but for this cause came I unto this hour. Father, glorify thy name. Then came there a voice from heaven, saying, I have both glorified it, and will glorify it again. The people therefore, that stood by, and heard it, said that it thundered: others said, An angel spake to him. Jesus answered and said, This voice came not because of me, but for your sakes. Now is the judgment of this world: now shall the prince of this world be cast out. And I, if I be lifted up from the earth, will draw all men unto me."* (John 12:27-32).

Many have thought this thirty-second passage means that if God is properly glorified in our preaching, then He will draw all people unto Himself. But that is not what this passage is saying. If you look in the King James Version, you will notice that the word "men" in verse 32 is italicized. That means it wasn't in the original language. The translators put this word in italics to let you know this was their addition, but it wasn't a part of the original text. If you take this verse in context, I believe that the Lord was saying He would draw all judgment to Himself.

It's time you drop your cross and take up His glory and the benefit of His death and resurrection.

Jesus, like a lightning rod, attracted all of God's judgment for all of mankind's sins for all time unto Himself. All the murder, all the perversion, every vile and rotten sin imaginable, all sickness, and all disease ever known to mankind actually entered into His physical human body. Isaiah 52:14 talks about the crucifixion of Jesus and says that He was marred more than any man to the point that He was unrecognizable as a human being.

That could not just happen from physical beatings, especially since the Word says that not a single bone was broken in His body (Psalms 34:20; John 19:36). I believe His body was completely disfigured from the cancers, tumors, diseases, deformities, and anything else human beings have ever suffered.

Jesus didn't ask for the cup to be taken from Him just because of the physical pain He would suffer but because He did not want to become sin. He hated becoming what He came to redeem us from. And the worst part of all Jesus' sufferings was total rejection from His Father. Matthew 27:46 says, *"And about the ninth hour Jesus cried with a loud voice, saying, Eli, Eli, lama sabachthani? that is to say, My God, my God, why hast thou forsaken me?"*

God the Father forsook Jesus so you and I would never be forsaken. All that you and I would have suffered, through billions of years in eternity—the grief, the pain and, worst of all, the complete separation from the presence of God—Jesus experienced. And He experienced all of this for us.

When we say God is judging our sins as individuals or corporately as a nation, we are voiding what Jesus did. That would be "double jeopardy." If Jesus has done all this for you, then why are you still carrying the cross He has conquered? Why are you still carrying that guilt, condemnation, and weight of sin around your neck? Why are you still trying to save yourself through your own works? Aren't you tied? I'm tired. I'm exhausted from all the religious rituals and always asking for forgiveness. I'm tired of trying to save myself. I have given up. Yes, that is right!! I have given up. Given up on what? on my ability in keeping the law, on my consistent asking for forgiveness, on my living like a slave whereas I have been chosen to reign on earth like a king.

I have dropped my cross and have taken up the glory of Jesus. I have dropped my cross and weight of sin and have taken up His nature. I have dropped my cross and taken up Jesus' righteousness, and it has been a beautiful experience and relationship with Jesus. I wish you could see me and His light and glory illuminating from within me.

Some folks may not like this, but it's true. Sin isn't a problem with God anymore. It's the church that has made it a major deal. Neither past, present, nor future sins can separate you from God. The only people who will go to hell are those who have spurned and rejected the greatest sacrifice that has ever been made. In heaven, you won't answer for your sin; Jesus already has. You will answer for your acceptance or rejection of Jesus.

You might now be thinking, "You're just giving people a license to sin." Well, it seems to me that people are doing a pretty good job of that without a license. What I'm saying does not free you to sin; it frees you from the condemnation and the guilt that comes when you do sin.

To continue in sin is just stupid. You'll be opening the door for Satan to have an inroad into your life (Romans 6:16). If you do, then you will suffer the natural consequences of sin, but it will not be because of the judgment of God.

If you commit adultery, you will probably lose your family, but it was you who caused it, not God. Natural disasters are just that—natural disasters. We live in a corrupted world where bad things happen, but God isn't the cause of them. If He were, why would He stop at New Orleans and the Gulf Coast of America? Surely all of us deserve the judgment of God. But, praise God, we don't get what we deserve.

Before I learned that the war was over, I used to say, "If God doesn't judge America and the rest of the Western world for all the homosexual acts, He will have to apologize to Sodom and Gomorrah." Now I say, "If God judges America, He will have to apologize to Jesus." Thank God for Jesus!

CHAPTER 15

WELCOME TO THE FAMILY OF GRACE

If you have been cast out, left out, wounded, broken, betrayed, or abused, this is your family. If you are weary of trying to save yourself, this is your family. If you are fed up with all the wrong teachings of religion and the law, this is your family. If you feel that religion and the law are just burdens for you to carry, then this is your family. If they have called you a sinner and a prostitute simply because you have a different style of fashion or because you like to enjoy the beauty of life like clubbing, partying, and vacationing, then this is your family.

In this family, there is no fault-finding; there is no condemnation; there is no envy or jealousy. In this family, there is no limit to your joy and happiness. In this family, you can be on fire for Jesus and still slay like the king or queen you are. In this family, you can be whomever you choose to be.

In this family of grace, Jesus wants to see you happy and enjoying the beauty of life. He is okay with you having a bottle or two bottles of beer. Hey, even when you get drunk, Jesus is still happy with you. Nevertheless, He wants you to be in good health, and that means being moderate in your drinking and eating habits. He is not saying you shouldn't drink your liquor; He is expecting you to drink responsibly.

This is a family of love. In this family, everyone is equal. There's no big or small, no high ranking nor low ranking, no more blessed or less blessed; for everyone is equal. Everyone is blessed and loved the same measure by God the Father. In this family, we were all battered and shattered with no hope of eternal life until Grace (Jesus Christ) saved us. What an amazing family.

In this family, guilt is not welcome, and we are all anointed in this family. This is the family for everyone. The LGBTQ are welcome into this family. Muslims are welcome into this family. Hindus are welcome into this family. Black, white, brown, whatever are all welcome into this family.

And you know the interesting thing? Everyone in this family has direct access to God the Father. Everyone is loved and cherished by Jesus, and He died for all of them. There is no discrimination or racism in this family, for love rules.

Experts at exclusion

Humanity has always found a way to choose one and exclude the other. Rewarding the good and punishing the bad. God, on the other hand, is not looking at humanity through the eyes of separation and exclusion. He doesn't see American and European, African and Asian, Hindu and Muslim, Christian and Buddhist. God sees humanity.

Traditional Evangelicalism has demanded that we create divisions and separations. Whether they are political, national, or religious, we really love our separating lines. They keep us comfortable. The message about God most of the world has heard is about a God of exclusion and separation. There seems to be this idea that God hates people until they believe in Him.

Well, what exactly are they supposed to believe about Him? That He loved them enough to die on the cross for their sins, of course. So, let me get this right...God hates people until they believe that God loves them? So, once people believe that God loves them, He then stops hating them and starts loving them?

Or how about this one...

"If God be for us, who can be against us?" (Romans 8:31b).

Who is the **"us"** in this passage? How do we become one of those included in this "us" group? "Well, we have to believe that it's true about us in order for it to be true about us," some would say. "So, God is for us when we believe that it's true about us." So, God is for us when we believe that He is for us? And before we believe it, God is against us? Does anyone else see a problem with this?

Before this verse, in Romans 5, Paul declared that God is for everyone, and that's why Jesus came and gave His life on our behalf, while we were still against Him. The pagans, Secularists, Muslims, Hindus, Humanists, New-agers, Homosexuals. Everyone.

We like to imagine that God is against these people. This gives us, "Christians" a reason to be against them. Of course, we say we aren't against these people. We are only against their ideologies. Unfortunately, it comes across much differently to a world that is waiting to see what God looks like.

Inevitably, we become what we worship. If we worship a God who is angry at humanity until they get their act together, then we will also be angry at people until they change. We will approach people in order to change them instead of to love and enjoy them. This is something that Jesus never did and never does. If Jesus waited for us to believe in His love before He loved us, then we'd all be in big trouble.

What if God is not against humanity? What if God loves everyone? What if Jesus cared about everyone regardless of what they believed about Him? What if God's love was unconditional? If you're like me, those questions put a smile on your face. I can't say that I've always been open to asking those questions, but that's part of growing and maturing...

Some of these thoughts are already stretching many of you. I commend you for being open to change and open to growth. You and I are still growing and still learning. So, let's hold on tight and keep reading, because the good news gets even better.

Jesus: Friend of The Weird and Non-Weird People

Can you imagine a God who is less like your local evangelical neighbor and more like Jesus? That sounds neat, but honestly, which Jesus are we talking about? Is it the one who is waiting for you to screw up so He can quickly convict you of sins? Is it the Jesus that spends most of His time at political rallies reminding people whom they should and shouldn't vote for? Is it the Jesus who is holding disgusting sinners over the pit of hell and can't wait to drop them if they don't repent? If that's the Jesus were talking about, then I think I'll pass. And the world has already passed.

Who in the world are we talking about? Well, let me share a few thoughts about who Jesus really is and what He is really like. Nowadays, Jesus has a pretty good reputation across the earth. Even among non-believers, Jesus is a respected Person. People usually don't like Christians, but they are open to Jesus because He seemed to do a lot of good.

Back in the day, the religious folks' view of Jesus was a little different. Luke 7:34 (NASB) reads, *"The Son of Man has come eating and drinking, and you say, 'Behold a gluttonous man and a drunkard, a friend of tax collectors and sinners."* He enjoyed feasting, He loved a good bottle of wine, and some of His best friends were known as sinners.

Jesus loved having fun. Does anyone else find it strange that the main reputation Christians carry usually has nothing to do with any of those things? Honestly, I'm not telling you that you must take up drinking if you don't want to. That's not the point. And if you love fasting, then go on with your hungry self.

But seriously guys, when was the last time you were accused of having too much fun? Or when was the last time you were accused of having too many bad friends? And I don't mean friends you only talk to during the outreach...I have a feeling Jesus was not mostly making friends with bad kinds just so He could convince them of how bad they were and how good He was. I think He enjoyed them. He wanted to hang out with them because He loved them and saw the beauty of their created value. His love and delight of them (not His preaching) is what changed them.

Here's a story to illustrate: Jesus shows up in town one day, and He is immediately mobbed by the crowd. Everyone was surrounding Him, hoping for a conversation, a prayer, or an embrace from the Man who was transforming the world. Somehow, Jesus was able to make everyone feel like the most important person in the world even with a simple glance in their direction. While hugging on the kids and smiling at the widows, he caught a glimpse of a dude hanging out in the trees – literally.

This guy, Zacchaeus, was about 5'5" and couldn't get a good glimpse of Jesus unless he climbed up into the tree – so that's exactly what he did. The rumors of Jesus – His disturbance of the religious system, the miracles He did, and how He was scorned by leaders as a "friend of sinners" – particularly made Zacchaeus curious.

Zacchaeus had never been a fan of the religious order, so if there was a dude out there like this, then he had to meet him. Zacchaeus was a tax-collector. This was not a very popular position to hold in the community back then (nor is it today). He used his position and power to make a little extra off almost everyone he collected from. Actually, let's just shoot straight. Zack stole from pretty much everyone. The guy was straight up gangster.

Religious leaders wouldn't be caught dead hanging out with a guy like Zacchaeus, unless it was for the purpose of telling him how much of an unclean sinner he was. Jesus, on the other hand, saw something completely different about Zack and told him that He would be going to his house.

Startled by the attention, Zacchaeus jumped down from the tree, "What?!? Party? I mean... I ...I... wasn't planning one, but I'm sure I could throw something together..." Jesus laughed as Zack stumbled over his words, and said, "Yeah, man... party at your place. Invite all your friends. We're gonna have a feast!"

Immediately, Zack came down from the tree and with tears in his eyes said, "Jesus, I would have never imagined You would accept me or pay any attention to me. Today, Lord, I am going to give ½ of everything I own to the poor. And, Lord, if I have stolen anything from anyone in this city, then I am going to pay them back four times as much as I have stolen! Today is a new day, and I feel like myself for the first time in a long time!"

Jesus looked at Zacchaeus. Then He looked at the people and said, "Zacchaeus has been forever changed today, and he's come to an understanding that he's my kid and not a product of the fallen world." No sermon. No picket signs. No declaration of hell and judgment. Zacchaeus was as saved as a saved person could be. All of this happened because Jesus preached a powerful sermon ... in fact it was the shortest and most powerful sermon in all of history.

For you preachers out there, here is the sermon in an outline form:

A. Hi, Zacchaeus.

B. I'm coming to hang out with you. No altar calls, no demand to "get right with God," only an abrupt moment of Jesus inviting himself over to the house of a dude who enjoyed stealing from people. This was enough to change this man's life.

Zacchaeus got saved because Jesus paid attention to him even though he was a modern-day gangster and extortionist. Jesus didn't mention his sin or his need for salvation; Jesus only told him that he wanted to grab dinner with him.

He treated Zacchaeus according to his "before the foundation of the earth" identity and not his current misguided lifestyle. The sermon was Jesus. The gospel is Jesus. There is no message outside of the Man. Seeing Jesus means seeing the God who is love incarnate: Love without expectations, love without demands.

When Jesus sees you, He doesn't see you through the lens of your mistakes and problems. He sees you according to the truth of how He created you. He sees you as a child of God. Jesus doesn't wait until people get right with Him before He spends time with us. If He did that, He never would have come in the first place.

The Bible says that Jesus is the friend of sinners. That means all of us. Being a "sinner" is not about how many bad deeds you've done. Being a sinner has to do with being identified with Adam's sin. We have all been identified with Adam's sin because we were all born from Adam. Jesus didn't reject Adam when he sinned, and Jesus doesn't reject us because of sin.

Holiness Expressed in Nearness

There's a verse in the Old Testament that seems to give this idea of God being so holy that He can't even look at our sin. Check it out: Habakkuk 1:13, (NRSV) reads, *"Your eyes are too pure to behold evil, and you cannot look on wrongdoing; why do you look on the treacherous, and are silent when the wicked swallow those more righteous than they?"*.

Habakkuk, well intentioned and sincere, still had little understanding of the character and nature of God. Sure, he was a prophet of God, but that doesn't mean he knew God. His confusion is expressed when he asks God about His ability to love, or even look at, sinners. "God, You are too holy to even look at sinners. So why in the world are you still putting up with them?"

I sympathize with Habakkuk. When all you see is bull crap happening around you, and you, of course, are keeping your act together by living holy, then it can start to get annoying that God is still putting up with all these sinners. I don't claim to know whether that was a real vision, but I do know one thing. If it was, then the folks who heard it misinterpreted it greatly. The only flesh Jesus calls stinking is the kind that makes us think that we have some part in making ourselves holy or keeping ourselves holy.

I have had Habakkuk's mindset before... until I realized that it was wrong. Interestingly, this verse has nothing to do with God being too holy to relate to bad people. In fact, it has more to do with the fact that God can and absolutely does look upon our sin and still loves His children.

God is not so clean that He can't get dirty. He's not so transcendent or far above us that He must look down in order to see us. In fact, in Christ, God declared that He is Emmanuel, God with us. When we think of God, we must think of Jesus. There is absolutely no separation between God the Father and the revelation of Jesus in the flesh. Anytime you hear something about God that does not line up with the life of Jesus Christ, then you can pretty much clamp it.

Look at what Paul said about Jesus: *"He is the image of the invisible God, the firstborn of all creation; for in him all things in heaven and on earth were created, things visible and invisible, whether thrones or dominions or rulers or powers--all things have been created through him and for him. He himself is before all things, and in him all things hold together."* (Colossians 1:15-17 NRSV).

Jesus is the exact representation of the Father. He is God, perfectly manifested in the flesh. In the person of Christ, we find our perfect reference for who God the Father always has been and always will be. God, being perfectly holy and pure, came in the form of Jesus and got down in the dirt with the worst of us, showing us what holiness looks like.

God found His best expression in the form of man – in Jesus Christ.

Holiness never has and never will have anything to do with living in a way that is separate from others. Holiness has its greatest expression in living a life of perfect love and enjoyment of those around us.

The holiness of God manifests in His nearness to us and His love for us. If that were not the case, the Pharisees (separatists) would have been the most God-like people on the planet when Christ came. But we know that wasn't the case. (*See* Matthew 23).

Think about this...

Before Jesus came, supposedly, mankind was evil, sinful, and unclean – unable to connect with God. But when Christ came, He had absolutely no problem hanging out and connecting with these evil and dirty people. Before anyone had prayed the sinner's prayer or repented, Jesus came, and He was not disgusted by us. Instead, He loved and enjoyed people and brought out the best in them.

Christ coming in the form of humanity was God's message to us that He has always been and will forever be connected to us. God didn't take a downgrade when He became human. Instead He took the form He loved deeply and was happy to be forever married to. God found His best expression in the form of man – in Jesus Christ.

I know what you are thinking "But, Great, the Bible says that 'sin separates us from God' so why are you saying that it doesn't?" We must interpret the types and shadows of the Old Covenant through the substance of the New Covenant. If you are viewing Christ through the lens of the prophets, then you have it backwards. We must interpret the prophets through the lens of Christ.

Who's Your Daddy?

I love the story of the prodigal son. You know, the story of the son who demanded his inheritance from his father then ran off and wasted it on cars, porn, prostitutes, and alcohol. Well, I've all too often heard preachers say that this story is about that "backslidden Christian" who needs to "come on home to the father tonight."

And, of course, at the end of the sermon, dozens of young people come streaming forward to rededicate their lives to Jesus. Don't get me wrong, that's fine and dandy, and I'm thankful that Jesus is preached. But all too often these kids just end up back in their so called "backslidden" lifestyles waiting for the next revival service to come around so they can pray that prayer again and "get right" with God one more time.

I used to preach the "prodigal son/backslidden Christian" message too... Well, that was until I realized that when Jesus shared this story, there was no such thing as a Christian (much less, a backslidden one). For some reason the church tends to think that they are the son that Jesus was talking about. Or that the church are the ones who were "in" and the rest of the world (those unbelieving outsiders) is nowhere to be found in this story.

I can't help but see the attitude of the church lining up more with the older brother in the story instead of the young prodigal. I guess we'll have to start at the beginning if we're ever going to get any clarity on who's in and who's out, who's God's kid and who's a reprobate bastard.

Christians are experts at coming up with systems, formulas, and labels. Systematic theology, formulas for faith, and labels for those who don't agree with us, all the while forgetting that trying to fit God into a system is like trying to... wait, there's nothing stupid enough to compare that with.

Formulas for faith? Well, that's just foolish. Labeling others? That only serves to put a box around them, so we feel comfortable shutting them out. Not to mention it gives us a filter through which to listen to them. What if God wasn't up in heaven looking at humanity as a divided family? What if from His vantage point, we were one? Relax...

I know that not everyone believes the same exact thing. But just because one of the kids in the family runs away from home doesn't mean that we are not all in the same family. It just means that kid needs to get fresh perspective of how great his parents are. Now, that's easy when you've got great parents and great brothers and sisters.

But when the parents want you home, but your brothers and sisters shun you for your mistakes and wrong thinking and say that you are not a part of the family until you "make things right," then that is definitely not very inviting. You already feel like trash, and they are just confirming your feelings of not belonging. What if the father accepted the son as a son even while he wasn't believing like a son or acting like a son? According to Jesus, that seems to be the case.

Back to the story of the prodigal son.... When that young son came groveling home on that bright sunny morning in July, he was fully expecting to give a speech of repentance and remorse while receiving a new role as a slave in the family. When he got home, he was hardly able to get past the "Hey Dad...sorry I screwed everything up," when his Dad told him to shut up and gave him a huge hug!

The son wanted to tell his Dad that he'd be sleeping in the barn tonight when suddenly Dad told him to head upstairs, and the servants would be getting his clothes ready for the party. The entire neighborhood was invited. Dad pulled out his debit card and gave it to the servant, telling him to go buy everything needed for a massive celebration. "And don't hold back on your spending; I want the best of everything for tonight," he demanded with a smile on his face.

Everyone came that night. It was wild – the biggest party the city had ever seen. Dad pulled out all the stops that night. Gave the kid a new wardrobe, upgraded his living situation at the house, surprised him with a brand-new Lamborghini, and told him he'd be taking the week off work to spend some quality time with him. Everyone had a blast, and they were all so grateful for the return of the son. Well, everyone except his older brother.

He left the party early and went to hang out in the basement, frowning and watching reruns of Full House on Netflix. When Dad noticed he wasn't around, he searched the house until he found him in the basement. "Buddy!" Dad said with a smile, (he had called him by this nickname since he was a kid). "You're missing all the action! Besides, you never hang down here... What's up?"

The older brother didn't take his eyes off the flat-screen, "Dad, seriously? Lamborghini? A party? New wardrobe? What the heck is going on!?" the brother asked with disdain. "Never once have I gotten a party this big and never once have you given me half of what you just gave this idiot son of yours who just came back from fornication, adultery, stealing, and squandering your money. I seriously wonder how you expect to see any change in him if you're just going to reward his stupid behavior like this!"

Dad cleared his throat and contained himself. "Wow son, I didn't know you felt this way. But, yes, you're right. We really did throw quite the party for this brother of yours," he said emphasizing the fact that they were brothers. "You know buddy," continues the daddy, "you and your brother have been close since you were kids. I really appreciate the way you've loved him and helped him out over the years. We both know that he's always had to learn the hard way in life, but that never made him any less of a brother to you or a son to me. "You both come from me, and nothing you both will ever do can change that. You're my kids and you are brothers. Besides that, the new Lamborghini? Are you serious? Dude, you can drive any one of the Beamers or Ferrari's whenever you feel like it! Just ask. Heck, just go drive it. They are all yours and his to take whenever you need. I've always made that clear to you! And if you want to take it with you when you move out, then feel free; it's yours! I mean, honestly, consider it all yours anyway. I trust you and I love you.

"Wipe that frown off your face and come celebrate, Buddy! Your brother was practically dead out there on the streets, and now he's home. I don't have time to make him feel bad for his decisions. He's been eating with pigs and feeling like one himself. That's enough punishment for one lifetime."

I think Jesus ended the story like this on purpose. The response is up to the reader. Of course, we all think that we are the prodigal son in this story. And sure, in some way we have all been that son. That's the point I'm making.

But I don't think it ended there. I have a feeling that we think we're at the party celebrating the son's homecoming, or our own, but we are all just hanging out down in the basement with one another watching Tiger King. The church enjoys the basement and the company of other brothers while we talk about how loud and blasphemous the party is upstairs. All the while, missing the real party that is all about the jacked-up younger brother that we call "that son of yours."

"There's no way that sinner is my brother, Great. I want nothing to do with him until he starts representing the family correctly in his beliefs and actions." Sound familiar?

The "Bad Guys" Who Do Good Stuff

Jesus told a story that has been popularized in Christian culture by the name "the good Samaritan." I never quite realized how scandalous this story must've been to those Jewish boys and girls who were listening to Jesus that day.

Those folks grew up hearing about the bad Samaritans down the road and how they were all going to be destroyed by God because they were so evil. These Samaritans were half Jews who didn't follow the customs of the Hebrews. They were the untouchable, the unclean, and the outcasts of society.

This was the reason Jesus was looked at outlandishly for speaking to the woman at the well. She was a Samaritan and a woman. Both things played against her in the social scheme.

Back to the story...It was quite awkward for Jesus to put a Samarian in His story and paint a good picture of him. The story begins with a man walking on a journey in the backwoods. On his way to the nearest city, the man gets robbed and beaten up by some street robbers and left for dead. While he was lying half-dead on the road, three men end up coming upon him.

First is the Rabbi. This teacher was in a hurry and had to get to his ministry meeting, so he had no time to stop to help this bloodied man. Next was a Levite, a good Israel-loving-conservative Levite. He was on his way to a meeting as well and had no time to stop and check on this man. So, he also passed right by the half-dead man.

The dude, still laying there bloodied and beaten, decided he'd just give up and die. I mean, if a Spirit-led Levite, and a pious pastor (Rabbi) from the local synagogue wouldn't stop to help, then no one would. As he pondered his last breaths, he was suddenly startled by a man stooping over him. "Are you okay?" said the man as he reached down to pick up the wounded man. Stunned, the little Jewish man realized it was a Samaritan who was reaching over to pick him up. "How could this be?" he thought to himself. "Dad always told me these guys were jerks."

Well, it turns out this Samaritan put the guy on his donkey and rode him to the nearest hotel. He put the guy up in a nice room and called the hospital. This ole' Samaritan paid the two-week hospital bill out of pocket, as well as his hotel stay. Can you imagine the mixed reactions of the crowd Jesus was speaking to? "No way! Not a dirty-Samaritan!" "Hmmm... I never would have thought..." "Wow... I knew those guys weren't so bad!"

Jesus knew all the buttons to push. So, he went after their deepest prejudice and kicked it where it hurt. "Love your neighbor as yourself" was the command that preceded this story, and, of course, He ended the story with this question: "Who was a neighbor to the injured man?" In other words, "Who fulfilled the command I just gave? Who, in this story, loved?"

The answer was obvious, yet a little disconcerting. What Jesus had just said was this: "The 'unclean' Samaritan just expressed the love of God to this man. He just treated this person as his neighbor the same way God treats everyone as His neighbor. Yes, the Samaritan who you are convinced is utterly depraved and can do no good, he is the one who expressed the fragrance of My Father. So, go and act like the Samaritan."

I have a feeling this is not hitting home with us. To make the story a little more relevant, just substitute the following characters and reread the story:

Rabbi = Local Pastor

Levite = Church Bible school teacher

Samaritan = Liberal-voting transvestite

Now that's better. For some people, that's not a big deal. But for those of you who have grown up in the world of the evangelical church, you know the implications of such a statement.

"So Great, what are you trying to say?" What I'm trying to say is that God's love, character, and nature can shine through those whom Christians often discount as dirty, sinful, and completely "unredeemed."

God's imprint and image is found on every human being and shines through them regardless of their awareness of it. Look at Jesus' response to the Pharisees in Luke 20:21-25 (ESV). *"So they asked him, 'Teacher, we know that you speak and teach rightly, and show no partiality, but teach the way of God. Is it lawful for us to give tribute to Caesar, or not?' But he perceived their craftiness, and said to them, 'Show me a denarius. Whose likeness and inscription does it have?' They said, 'Caesar's.' He said to them, 'Then render to Caesar the things that are Caesar's, and to God the things that are God's.'"*

Jesus seems to always answer questions with even better questions. The key to understanding Jesus' final answer about the coin lies in understanding His question to the Pharisees: whose image is on the coin? These guys had no idea where Jesus was going with this. They went ahead and answered him, "Caesar's of course."

You Have Arrived

Folks are tired of seeing the damned pictures and hearing ideas of a mystical heaven that seem to have almost nothing in common with the concrete reality. And the message of hell which has done more to push people away from God than bringing them to Him.

I have met wonderful people who, due to wrong teachings and false misrepresentation of the nature and personality of God, have concluded they'd rather go to hell with their friends than hang out in heaven with a God who sends people to hell. I don't blame them. But this is not who my loving Father is. I do believe in a literal heaven, and I do believe in a literal hell. But I do not and will not espouse to a definition of the gospel that has more to do with heaven and hell than it does with the Person and work of Jesus Christ on the cross.

Religion has falsely misrepresented
the nature and personality of God.

We haven't only been saved from a future hell through Jesus' death, but we have been protected from a present hell. The state of living in a constant sham about the character and nature of God, believing that He is the god who is against us, is a living hell itself.

Adam's fallen mind and the fallen nature passed on through his fruit binge was the initial taste of present hell that we all inherited. But Christ and His sabotage of our sinful existence was the solution that brought us to the now reality of our heavenly experience.

We have been seated with Christ in heavenly places. (Ephesians 2:6). We have been made partakers of the divine nature. (2 Peter 1:4). We have been hidden in Christ and absorbed completely in God (Colossians 3:1-3). As much as we enjoy talking about the future, I feel like we often miss the truth about present. The deific message is less about the future hope and more about a present reality that only gets better and better and goes from glory to glory. Don't get me wrong. Yes, it is about the future. But it is just as much about now.

All we have is now, the present. That's why the Apostle Paul wrote *"Today is the day of salvation."* (2 Corinthians 6:2c). It's pointless to get hung up on the future because all that we truly have within our grasp is today, right now. We are only going from glory to glory, from now to now, and thankfully, Christ is within us now, and He is the now expectation of our today glory and our future glory. (*See* Colossians 1:27).

The Apostle Paul and the other Apostles never relegated God's news to the future possibility of what we will get if we do our best to be good Christians. Instead, the message was a declaration of something that God did on our behalf that we get to take part in through our simple recognition that we have all been included in His love.

Our future is something we partake in by partaking in today. Many relegate heaven, perfection, and freedom from the sinful nature to a day far away, something that we will eventually attain when we die. But, if death is our freedom from imperfection, then go ahead and consider yourself dead.

This is what Paul said about this issue, check it out: *"Even so consider yourself to be dead to sin, but alive to God in Christ Jesus."* (Romans 6:11, NASB). Colossians 3:3 (NASB) reads, *"For you have died and your life is hidden with Christ in God."*

The declaration of our salvation is about what has been done through the work of Christ. He became our sinful self, our imperfect self, and we became His perfection. The Scriptures say, He made Him who knew no sin to be sin on our behalf, so that we might become the righteousness of God in Him." (2 Corinthians 5:21, NASB). When He died on the cross, our imperfect self, died along with Him. All our failures died. All our mistakes, past, present, and future, were crucified with Him. All our negative emotions were buried once and for all.

Perfection Has Been Paid For

Friend you're perfect! You are!! It's your heritage. It had been given to you permanently through Jesus Christ, and there is nothing the enemy or anyone can do about it. Let no one deceive you with man's philosophies and theologies. Hebrews 10:14, NASB reads, *"For by one offering He has perfected for all time those who are sanctified."*

You Are Perfect. Completeness has been given freely to you. These are not my words or some wisdom. This is what the Scriptures say about you. *"For in Him all the fullness of Deity dwells in bodily form, and in Him you have been made complete."* (Colossians 2:9-10a, NASB).

You Are Complete. God dealt with sin. The false reality that there is another way to live in perfection outside of friendship with Him is just an indicator of someone who lacks scriptural understanding. It is the deception of self-effort and the lie that says humanity has effects.

Perfection is not a destination
but rather a person, and
Jesus Christ is that perfection.

It is a lie that Man wasn't made perfect, and that we were not good. But God made Man and declared: "It is good." Somewhere along the way, we stopped believing that and started trying to become good. Sure, sin tainted us, but before sin had tainted us, Jesus sainted us. Ephesians 1:4 (NASB) *reads, "He chose us in Him before the foundation of the world, that would be holy and blameless before Him."*

Sin could never steal our origin, and it could never change our design. Mankind's problem was in our head. We believed the lie that we lacked something, so we gave in to the deception to try and gain something. When we did this, we entered a lower domain of unbelief, and our understanding was darkened by deception. Our eyes became evil and darkened, and the world we saw, we saw through a darkened lens of unbelief.

Unbelief in what? In God's goodness, in our origin, and in our eternal identity as His children. We began seeing our Father as a judge and our Friend as a foe. God saw fit to come and deal with this darkened understanding, this Adamic idea. So, He came in the form of weakened and feeble Mankind, susceptible to our sin and brawl, yet walking in complete victory over our darkened mindsets. He came and became our brokenness in order to destroy it once and for all.

In Jesus Christ, you are complete; you are forgiven all your sins. In Christ Jesus, you have eternal life. Beloved, the veil was torn on your behalf. No more condemnation, no more guilt. You are saved. You are righteous. You are perfect. This is your new identity in Christ.

The wages of your sins – past, present, and future – have been paid for by Jesus Christ's death on the cross. You are righteous in the eyes of God. This is the good news friend. It's finished...Welcome to the family of Grace, where Jesus Christ's death, burial, and resurrection is the only message we teach and listen to. The veil is indeed torn, the partition has been lifted from before us, now drop your cross, through away all those guilt and self-condemnation and receive His life.

HERE IS ENCOURAGEMENT DURING THIS COVID-19 PANDEMIC

Friends, this virus is here. It's brutal, and it's has dealt with us as a community, as a State, and as a nation in terrible ways. Many have lost loved ones, fathers, mothers, grandparents, spouses, children, and friends.

Throughout the first quarter of this virus, many lost their jobs and consequently entered unforeseen financial challenges. But I tell you beloved, this virus may be strong, but we are stronger. We are resilient, and together in love we will defeat this enemy from the pit of hell. There is nothing we cannot do or achieve as a nation if we join our hands together against a common enemy.

But to achieve this goal, we have to each play our small part in helping to stop the spread of this virus through keeping the stipulated social distancing guidelines of 6ft, washing our hands, wearing facemasks as often as we can, and avoiding crowded place or events. Yes, the government is easing the lockdown, but if we don't adhere to these necessary preventive measures outlined by the CDC, more people will die, especially our aging population.

Believe me, I know these precautionary measures are sometimes discomforting. I know some people have complained that it's difficult to breathe while wearing the facemask, but come on, guys. It will be worse if you contract the virus or worse spread it to people unconsciously. You might say, "Hey, Great, I don't have the virus!" Well, as true as that may be, our healthcare professionals and scientists have told us that one could be asymptomatic yet contagious, meaning you might not show symptoms of the virus but still be a carrier of it, spreading it unknowingly.

I believe that God has given our doctors and scientists out there the wisdom and ideas needed to develop a vaccine that will neutralize and end this coronavirus once and for all. This is my confidence and I invite you to join your faith with mine as we continue to pray while watching the miracle happen.

Also, I have seen on the news and some social media platforms out there that even some highly respected religious leaders are spreading conspiracy theories about the virus – it's the product of 5G network; it was developed in the laboratory somewhere in China; it's the end of the world; the vaccine is a means to initiate a new world order. As much as this might sound so cool and believable, considering what is going around the world, friend, I encourage you to listen to experts and search for truth from credible and reliable sources.

I know those statements are false. They are all conspiracy theories on dark web aimed to drive fear and chaos in the minds of people and our communities. I'm not a scientist nor a doctor, but I'm knowledgeable enough to know that virus, bacterial, and other forms of disease exist. This planet is ours, and no one is taking it from us. Neither is God angry with the world and using this coronavirus to wipe us out. Like we discussed in this book, God loves us and will never destroy us. He is our Father; we are His beloved children.

Our Church buildings are temporarily closed because we need to avoid large gatherings, so many people are missing the fun of going to church, listening to the beautiful choir sing their favorite songs, listening to the pastor preach, and just meeting friends generally. But I'd like you to know that you are the church of God. The church is not a building. The church is you. You are the temple of God. Although the buildings where we gather to fellowship together are closed, God is ever with you, and you can worship Him anywhere, including your house or apartment.

One reason we must develop a personal relationship with Jesus and not just going to church every Sunday is so at times like this, we don't get spiritually stranded or feel empty because no pastor is there to preach to us. You need to know Jesus for yourself. God is not interested in your magnificent and elegant 20 thousand-seater church building, He is interested in you. You are His temple. You are the reason He died, not your building. So, stop building your Christian life around your church. Build it around Jesus and the Word of God. (See Matthew 18:20)

Lastly, I would like to give a shout out to all our Doctors, Nurses, Medical assistants, Janitors, first responders, and the Sales Representatives in the various Groceries Stores who are putting their lives in danger treating all those who have been infected by the coronavirus or just making sure we have food on our tables. You are my heroes. You all, are the SUPERMAN, CAPTAIN AMERICA and WONDER WOMAN of these troubling times. May God continue to protect and bless you all for your service. Honestly, no salary can compensate for the risk you are all taking on our behalf during this pandemic.

GETTING IN TOUCH WITH ME...

Hey, like to contact Great Igwe, for Bookings, Mentorship, Counselling or questions and clarity on any topic in this book, you can do so by:

Email: greatigwe28@gmail.com

Website: www.greatigwe.com

OR

Follow Pastor Great on:

@Greatigwe2

@Greatigwe

@Greatigwe

NOTES